"A biblical perspective on
A must-read."

KATIE BRAZELTON, PhD, MDiv, MA
Best-selling author and founder of
Life Purpose Coaching Centers International®

"If you need some encouragement, inspiration, affirmation—
or even a gentle little push—to take a risk and become a better
leader than you currently are, then this book is for you!"

MARY KASSIAN
Author, *Girls Gone Wise*

"This book will awaken you to the reality that you *can* lead
and you *do* lead even if, like me, you've never seen yourself as a
leader. *Unlocked* will open your eyes to the leadership potential
and positions in your own life. If you've been looking for some
'giddy-up,' Cynthia Cavanaugh's book has what you need.

—CONNIE CAVANAUGH, speaker and author of *Following God One Yes
at a Time* and *From Faking It to Finding Grace,* conniecavanaugh.com

UNLOCKED

5 Myths Holding
Your Influence Captive

CYNTHIA CAVANAUGH

NEW HOPE
PUBLISHERS
Gospel-Centered Missions-Driven.

BIRMINGHAM, ALABAMA

New Hope® Publishers
P. O. Box 12065
Birmingham, AL 35202-2065
NewHopeDigital.com
New Hope Publishers is a division of WMU®.

Library of Congress Control Number: 2013940551

Cover and Interior Design: Glynese Northam

ISBN-10: 1-59669-385-1
ISBN-13: 978-1-59669-385-2

N134126 • 0813 • 3M1

Dedication

To my grandparents, who lived out their faith impressing upon a young girl's heart to engage her ordinary life with an extraordinary God, and to embrace the adventure.

"You make known to me the path of life; you will fill me with joy in your presence, with eternal pleasures at your right hand."

PSALM 16:11

TABLE OF CONTENTS

Acknowledgments

Writing a book doesn't happen through just one person. Although the author's name is on the cover, what is woven through the pages is a community of relationships that have brought the writing to life. First of all, I want to thank the many women who have allowed me to tell their stories. Many have been my friends, and I have had the privilege to watch them grow and flourish. I have laughed, cried, and celebrated with them. Others I have watched from a distance and marvel at their courage and tenacity. In every case, I am richer because of learning from their obedience to follow God's call no matter what. Their leadership has influenced me. They have inspired me to love deeper and to take risks even if I am afraid. They are truly my heroes. Thank you for allowing me to share your stories of faith and leading from a place of real life.

I want to thank New Hope® Publishers for pursuing and believing in this book and encouraging me at every step of the process. It has felt like family from the beginning.

I want to thank my sons and their wives, Jeremy and Emily, Jordan and Julie, Jason and Brittany. I have learned so much about leadership from each of you. You have given me room and grace the past few years to learn some of the most challenging lessons. Thank you for your love and encouragement.

I want to thank my two little grandsons, Connor and Tyson. I have learned so much about who God is through your eyes.

I love to spend time with you! You've reminded me not to take life so seriously and make time to laugh and play.

I want to thank my church family for modeling servant leadership and giving me opportunities to serve the body of Christ with my leadership gifts. You have been a true family, embracing both the wonderful and the sometimes extremely difficult, and still loving Kevin and me unconditionally as your leaders. I will be eternally grateful.

I want to thank my husband, Kevin, who never stopped believing and encouraging me as a writer and who reminded me that I have words to share that matter to others. Thank you for being my cheerleader.

Lastly, I want to thank my Father and Lord Jesus Christ. It is only because of You that I have anything worthwhile to say. I have been tested and tried and have found You, Jesus, to be more than faithful. You are writing the story, and it is a privilege and honor to bring You glory in the pages of my life.

INTRODUCTION

Countless women are serving in leadership roles, but many of them don't refer to themselves as leaders. *Why?*

False ideas and unrealistic expectations of leadership restrain them from aspiring to and reaching the dreams God has for them and those they influence. If I had a dollar for every time I have heard women talk about their inadequacies and insecurities about leading, I would be able to buy a resort property! After I probe them a bit and ask them about their personalities and gifts, I find to no surprise that God is using them, as ordinary women, to do extraordinary assignments. When I tell them they are leading, they look at me cross-eyed and laugh!

After several years and many conversations with women in leadership, I took an informal survey from across my sphere of influence to ask, *Why do women run away from stepping up to all that God asks of them, especially if it is in the realm of being called a leader?* From the survey of nearly 100 leaders came a common thread: five myths—reasons why women don't see themselves as leaders or can't embrace leadership.

My hope is that the woman who picks up this book is a woman who is daring to be more than she is currently. She just needs a little push—or shove in some cases—to take a risk and step up to the assignment God has purposed for her life. She is hoping to find maybe just a little bit of encouragement, inspiration, and affirmation. Prayerfully reading the accounts of women in Scripture, as they are linked to each chapter, will help her to engage a confident, godly attitude that can be displayed in various areas of her life and leadership. I like to think of women as being agents of change through influence, so I am calling the woman who reads this book to think of herself as a *woman of influence*. She might lead a small group, be a stay-at-home mom, be a woman in the marketplace, be the women's ministry director in her church, work in an office, be in management, lead in a Christian organization, or anything somewhere in between.

What you will find in the following pages is my invitation to dispel the myths that paralyze women's ability to glorify God through their influence and leadership roles. My hope is that you will embrace the real stories of women who at one time or another struggled with leadership but rose up to accept the assignment God was calling them to do. I long for God to unravel the mysteries in your own heart as you read, to reaffirm and unlock the unimaginable leader God has designed you to be! And by the way, I would even invite my male friends who want to have a greater glimpse into a woman's heart to keep reading. Who knows? You may find part of your own story to empower and encourage the women in your life.

I AM NOT ENOUGH

Myth 1

Chapter 1

Leading from a Place of
Risk and Uncertainty

RAHAB

"Great deeds are usually wrought at great risks."
—HERODOTUS

"There are risk and costs to a program of action.
But they are far less than the long-range risks and
costs of comfortable inaction."
—JOHN F. KENNEDY

Several years ago, just a few blocks from a rundown part of town, a makeshift mobile kitchen was set up on the edge of a grassy lawn. Since that time, every night of the year devoted volunteers serve and feed people who have found themselves on the fringe of society. They are often cold, unwashed, and suffer from a variety of stigmas. Others might call them homeless, rejects, jobless, addicts, or losers. And yet something very meaningful happens each and every night; actually, you might call it a small miracle. The recipients of this kindness receive a warm smile with a hug or a handshake, but more importantly, they receive hope.

MaryAnne Connor was a successful real estate marketing executive living in an upscale community. In 2004, in response to a severe cold-weather warning, she rallied recruits to minister to the "least of these" in her city by providing shelter, food, and clothing for people living on the streets. From this one evening the vision for NightShift Street Ministries was born. In the early days of the ministry MaryAnne went as far as to spend a few nights in the cold huddled under a storefront with her "street friends," as she calls them, who regularly make the doorways and streets their home.

NightShift Street Ministries has come a long way from those days. Today more than 30 churches and more than 2,000 volunteers in the community take turns serving so that every single night people can be fed and given assistance so they might stay off the streets. NightShift is not just a soup kitchen or a bandage. Those who join MaryAnne and the mission create change. Mac, as MaryAnne is affectionately called on the streets, is a vibrant, petite, blonde woman who has chosen a life contrary to just settling for a comfortable, successful career. She is passionate in her pursuit of creating a ministry that renews the dignity of the human soul in some of the most adverse circumstances. I have often heard MaryAnne say that she doesn't know how the next step of Nightshift will be accomplished, but she confesses that she knows the One who does and therein lies her trust. Her feelings of inadequacy and uncertainty only fuel her determination to rely on God to move the ministry forward.

NightShift Street Ministries has grown from a mobile soup kitchen to a permanent site with offices, a training center for volunteers and leaders, the Care Project (which includes a counseling center), the Care Bus (a mobile medical unit), and steps toward a first-stage Care Cottage to help people move off the streets and back into society as healthy and whole individuals. Most importantly, the thread of this ministry is extending Christ's love and sharing the hope of the gospel for restoration and healing. The mission of the ministry is to *love unconditionally and help others find hope and purpose.* MaryAnne has embraced the truth that we are not enough in and of ourselves and that dreams happen as a result of taking risks in the midst of our own insecurities. She often confesses when she shares the story of NightShift, "If God can accomplish extraordinary things through a person like me, He can do the same through you."

Once Upon a Time

> MaryAnne is a woman who has definitely shattered our first myth of I Am Not Enough.

MaryAnne's story of brokenness drives her to be a voice for the shunned and forgotten. She is a single woman who is a mom, grandmother, friend, daughter, and ministry leader fulfilling many roles to which women can relate. Her determination challenges me. I stand in awe of her willingness to listen to God and leave a status quo lifestyle to hang out with those that—let's face it—some of us wouldn't look in the eye when we pass by.

Yet MaryAnne lived a "once upon a time" life before God dropped NightShift Street Ministries into her heart and hands.

Once upon a time is a phrase familiar to all of us. It marks the beginning of a fairy tale. I am not ashamed to admit I like fairy tales. They are neat and tidy stories with happy endings. They transport me into a world that seems perfect and desirable. There is a problem, however, with believing fairy tales: they don't translate so well to real life. They end up creating what I like to refer to as the Cinderella syndrome, perpetuating unrealistic expectations and the pursuit of perfection.

Admittedly, I have been guilty of having this attitude. At times I have slipped and allowed my mind and actions to reflect mistaken thinking that A should always lead to B and then life would fall neatly into place.

Really? *How could I be so naive?* Life is messy. And no matter how hard we try, it is complicated and simply doesn't work out the way we think it should. This thought pattern has manifested itself most significantly in how I view myself as a person, which in turn has an impact on how I see myself as a leader, and at times has kept me from taking risks—for fear of finding myself inadequate.

Talking with other women and listening to their stories, I have found that I am not alone. I have discovered that most women struggle with living up to a false idea and myth of what a godly leader looks like in their church or community. "I don't know if I can do this" is a statement I have heard count-less women make, including myself at times. It is this type of self-talk that sabotages our ability to take action when God whispers a cause or need into the depths of our beings.

Even as I approached writing this book on women in leadership, my mind suddenly became a tangled web of negative thoughts and lies. The thought *I can't do this!* crossed my mind. I now recognize the deception of the enemy who would love to paralyze my ability to fulfill God's desire to use me as a leader.

I have come to the conclusion that we often wrestle with emotions like these *as we serve in leadership roles* because most women don't have the luxury of focusing on *just* being a leader. Life is continually changing for us, and it affects how we function; first as women and then in the various parts we play, so we feel inadequate.

Very few women who are career leaders have been granted enormous chunks of time to focus on leadership. We are multitasking women. We are wives, mothers, grandmothers, caregivers, students, volunteers, and a plethora of other roles. We can't always spend an eight-hour day concentrating on specific leadership tasks. Multiple interruptions and numerous "have-to" tasks press in around us, shrieking for our attention.

We sometimes fall into the trap of settling for living out our various roles while feeling empty, and even taking on roles that God never intended for us. We then miss the opportunities and misunderstand what it means to live out our calling within the roles God has already entrusted to us.

The confusion of multitasking roles, coupled with our thoughts of inadequacy, can limit us from responding to a severe weather warning as Mac did because we just can't figure out all the steps. I have a news flash for you: We aren't supposed to know all the steps! God asks us to consider Psalm 37:7, "Be still before the Lord and wait patiently for him." Or as another translation states, "Wait expectantly" (HCSB). We are to believe by faith that God will reveal the next step of the journey.

If you have a dream for God, a pressing ache in your heart in an area of need that won't go away but keeps you awake at night, and you can't figure out how to make it happen, then it may be a dream that God wants you to jump out and take a risk as a leader. As you wait expectantly, He will tell you the appropriate moment to put your little frightened toe in the Jordan River and watch the waters of opportunity part. Isn't that what faith is all about?

Does that mean we abandon our assigned primary roles such as being a wife, mother, student, caregiver, or employee? Absolutely not! God will never ask you to step out and take a risk that would jeopardize a priority to which He has already called you.

You can count on the fact that God will be faithful to help you to take a God-given risk according to His purpose and design for your life. Your job is to listen for His signal and then *just do it*, despite feelings of inadequacy or uncertainty.

UNCALCULATED RISK IN A DESPERATE TIME

Rahab was a desperate woman. She was a prostitute living in Jericho, a city that was about to be demolished by God through Joshua and His army. She had a choice to make that would change her life and the lives of those she loved. She took an enormous risk and hid the spies Joshua had sent in preparation for capturing and destroying the great city. When the king's messenger came looking for them, she calmly lied and said that the spies had left the area. Here is her conversation with those spies:

Before the spies lay down for the night, she went up on the roof and said to them, "I know that the Lord has given this land to you and that a great fear of you has fallen on us, so that all who live in this country are melting in fear because of you. We have heard how the Lord dried up the water of the Red Sea for you when you came out of Egypt, and what you did to Sihon and Og, Amorites east of the Jordan, whom you completely destroyed. When we heard of it, our hearts melted and everyone's courage failed because of you, for the Lord your God is God in heaven above and on the earth below. Now then, please swear to me by the Lord that you will show kindness to my family, because I have shown kindness to you. Give me a sure sign that you will spare the lives of my father and mother, my brothers and sisters, and all who belong to them, and that you will save us from death."

"Our lives for your lives!" the men assured her. "If you don't tell what we are doing, we will treat you kindly and faithfully when the Lord gives us the land."

> *So she let them down by a rope through the window, for the house she lived in was part of the city wall. Now she had said to them, "Go to the hills so the pursuers will not find you. Hide yourselves there three days until they return, and then go on your way"* (Joshua 2:8–15).

Rahab may not have calculated the danger of the risk she took. She didn't really have the time to think about her inadequacies; her own life and family were at stake. If you read between the lines, her confession of belief in the Almighty God was enough for her to practice taking a step of faith. That faith was so great that she is honored in the "hall of faith" (Hebrews 11:31). James says this about Rahab: "In the same way, was not even Rahab the prostitute considered righteous for what she did when she gave lodging to the spies and sent them off in a different direction?" (2:25). The story doesn't end there. Rahab became the wife of Salmon, one of the princes of Judah, and the mother of Boaz, King David's grandfather!

Here is where I am headed with this: God yearns to honor the faith of anyone who believes Him enough to act and chooses to take a risk. The bottom line is, can you and I exercise Rahab risk-taking faith? What are we waiting for?

SETTLING FOR THE SHALLOW

I love the church. I love women. I believe women are called to serve in significant roles, and in doing so have the capacity to have an impact and influence godly change. When I talk to women, even some women in leadership, I am saddened that so many of them settle in defeat, taking on only roles they feel adequate in. Our world needs more—our world needs women who will go into the unknown, embracing inadequacy and counting their particular inadequacies as assets rather than as deficits. Wouldn't that be a new concept? That we as women could actually seize the idea that our deficits could actually work toward our favor.

If we were to host a gathering of women leaders and share our individual leadership journeys, many of us would confess that we didn't wake up one day aspiring to lead in the way we find ourselves presently leading. Most of us would admit that we are ordinary women whom God one day nudged in the direction of leading an event, a small group, or a life-changing action like NightShift Street Ministries. Some of us could even say we don't even know how we landed into leadership as we look back, baffled at the process.

The enemy's strategy hasn't changed since he succeeded in confusing and tempting Eve in the garden. He isn't very creative and continues to offer us a shallow way of life in having us "settle," deceiptfully seeking to convince us that we need to "be more" to be effective and productive.

Like the story of Rahab, our world is desperate to be rescued, for the foundations of decent society are crumbling. This is a time of moral corruption, complacency, and a reluctance to know and understand godly truth. Sadly, it has even crept into the church.

God is calling you and me as women, His daughters, and His princesses, to rise up. He is appealing for us to embrace a godly, confident attitude in our leadership as we serve, and not to linger over thoughts that whisper, *I can't do this.* Pablo Picasso once said, "I am always doing that which I cannot do, in order that I may learn how to do it."

Part of risking is learning in the realm of the unknown, even when we wrestle with feelings of *I AM NOT ENOUGH.* That is the key to the vault of treasure, to thrust open the gates and live and dare to risk, for if we do not risk, we do not truly live.

Father, I confess I often feel inadequate, that I AM NOT ENOUGH. *That's a good thing when I put it into perspective to work in partnership with You. I don't always know how to fulfill what You have assigned to me. I surrender those thoughts that seek to paralyze and keep me from acting out Your will for my life. Give me a brave heart; infuse me with courage to take uncalculated risks—by faith. Lead me, Jesus, to a place of complete trust as I take a step of faith toward following Your destiny for my life. Amen.*

Chapter 2

Leading with Authenticity

THE SAMARITAN
WOMAN

*Authenticity is a collection of choices that
we have to make every day.
It's about the choice to show up and be real.
The choice to be honest.
The choice to let our true selves be seen.*
—Brené Brown, author, *The Gift of Imperfection*

I don't like fake flowers, fake snow at Christmas, fake leather, fake fur (although I do own a coat with some fake fur on it!), or fake anything for that matter. In relationships, I struggle when the other person expresses fake emotions or puts on pretense in order to disguise his or her true personality.

I haven't always felt so strongly about the word *fake* and its implications in relationships. There was a time in my life as a younger leader that I was afraid to reveal my true self. I thought that if those I was leading saw anything but confidence and strength, they would think less of me. I felt I would lose their respect and their desire to be led. I soon discovered that I couldn't keep up that facade for too long.

Early in my ministry I was leading worship for a women's retreat. On Saturday night, I was asked to lead a worship response to the message the speaker would be sharing. I asked her for specifics, which was my first mistake, because when I found out what she would be teaching, I ran scared! She had been leading us through a series of emotions that women struggle with, and in the evening she had planned on teaching about anger. In my room preparing before the session, God strongly suggested to me (in a persistent, quiet whisper) that if I wanted the women to respond to the message through worship and sharing, I would have to lead the way. Drat! I knew this was going to happen, and I wasn't quite ready for it just yet. I tried to ignore it, but God wouldn't leave me alone. He kept my attention through the ring of truth I was sensing in the deep place of my soul. I hadn't quite conquered the anger in my life, and I certainly didn't want anyone to know, let alone nearly 150 emotional women at the retreat.

During the session the impression in my heart was so strong that as I sat at the desk, my hands were clammy and my heart was racing. The speaker finished her message. I began to lead in worship, and then as I opened it up for sharing, I stopped. I confessed my insecurity and my inadequacy and removed the mask I was wearing. I let the women know that night I was a real person who struggled with anger. What followed was beyond what I expected. What happened opened the door for women to share their own secret struggles and need for healing. There were tears, prayers, and a closing song of triumph as our hearts sang in unison, realizing we were all in this together. We were women who needed Jesus in the messiest parts of our lives. That night was a spiritual marker for me. I didn't want to be real. The one comment someone said to me later I will never forget, "I am so glad you shared. You see, I never felt I could even talk to you because you seemed so perfect. Now I know I am OK!"

Part of believing the myth I AM NOT ENOUGH, keeps us from being our true selves. Our insecurities and inadequacies can drive us to wearing a mask for fear of someone finding out the truth of who we really are. As a leader, if we aren't willing to reveal who we are, then there is no room for viable ministry. Being authentic as a leader gives those who follow permission to do the same, and the result is a team of people who recognize their need for God. When you are truly authentic it is a part of knowing and being OK with the thought that you are not enough.

BECOMING FEARFULLY AUTHENTIC

Being authentic is frightening for some people. OK, to be real, it's disheartening for me. I referred in the first chapter to donning an attitude I like to call the Cinderella syndrome. As a little girl, I fantasized about Cinderella. Maybe because my grandmother acted out the story when I was in her care. She became the fairy godmother, the wicked stepmother and sisters, the handsome prince; and I, of course, always played the part of Cinderella. Having the nickname Cyndi, my father to this day still calls me his Cinderella. Growing up, I went from playing Cinderella to believing the lie that the kind of perfection and idealism portrayed in that story could actually translate into real life. When real life turned out differently, I hid my true emotions and thoughts, thinking others would see me as a failure and choose not to invite me to the coveted ball. It wasn't until my mid-30s that hiding my failures, my faults, and my imperfections actually drove me to a crisis. I sank into a clinical depression in which I had no place to hide because it radically limited my ability to function. I had no choice but to surrender and allow God to minister to me in the deepest caverns of my soul and allow others to enter my pain. Because this is a chapter about being authentic, it seems only fitting that I share this journey. It is never easy for me to crack open the vault of my soul, but I have come to surrender to God's call to tell the truth so others will follow. My deepest hope is that it will encourage you on your own journey of authenticity.

The Black Hole

My journey with depression began early in the spring of 1997— that's when I had been diagnosed with clinical depression. Long days and weeks of caring for my grandfather had taken its toll. Blackness and despair sought to submerge me. The diagnosis of depression, though, was difficult for me to digest. I could swallow a diagnosis of arthritis or diabetes, but depression? In my mind, depression was for weak people and weak Christians who didn't have enough faith. I argued about the diagnosis with

God, my counselor, pastor, and doctor, all people who were trying to help me. *I am a visible leader, a pastor's wife in the church. What will people whisper about me behind closed doors if they know?* I worried. The lies flooded my mind and I was overwhelmed at being exposed.

As my desert of depression continued over the next few years, I discovered that the depression wasn't just from the losses I had experienced the past several months. Nor was it from my physical exhaustion. Actually, I learned it was from deeper issues that had been tucked away—issues that God was beginning to bring to the surface. Some of those issues included false expectations and a warped perspective of needing to perform in order to be lovable. Those lies were sabotaging me and had plunged my spiritual and emotional being into the black hole of depression. I started to learn that performance had a stronghold in my heart, life, and ministry that God in His faithfulness desired to root out. Through my counselor I realized that my depression was a symptom of something deeper, something below the waterline that must be faced in order to be a whole person again.

My good friend, who was also my counselor, helped me significantly when she used this illustration: If I had a broken leg, would I lie on the sofa, not tell anyone, and just hope it would heal? No! I would go to the doctor immediately to get treatment. The same must be true for depression; a person often needs professional, spiritual, and medical help to overcome their extreme feelings of despair and hopelessness. Through professional help, they will be able to explore the root of what is causing the depression so they once again can lead a life of joy and fulfillment! That is how I came out of hiding into the realm of living in freedom and authenticity.

I can remember struggling alone at first because of the fear of rejection, failure, or being told, "If your faith was stronger, you wouldn't be depressed." (Believe it or not, I was told similar statements!) I know that I have been more fortunate than some and was blessed mostly to have a body of believers who came around and supported me. I thank God that the churches I served at as a leader in that season didn't see my depression as a sign of weakness or spiritual failure. Rather they sought to help me to a path of healing.

The undeniable reality of being in that black hole was both devastating, and yet it opened the door to living in emotional health and freedom. It radically changed my ministry approach and defeated the lies of rejection. In fact, it triggered the opposite. As a leader, it cultivated a leveling place of humility in experiencing God's abundant grace. It has built bridges with hundreds of women and provided opportunities to help women recognize that God wants to use their past to shape their future. It has opened the door and allowed me to be a cheerleader for women who thought that God could never allow them to lead.

FALLACY OF A FAIRY TALE

Whenever God prompts me to tell my depression journey it leaves me emotionally bankrupt. I would much rather retreat into a cozy land of make-believe. I sometimes imagine life would be simpler if it played out more like a fairy tale. As much as I adore the Cinderella-type fairy tales, one flaw that cannot be overlooked—the lie that many women buy into. It's the lie that keeps women from believing Ephesians 3:20: "Now to him who is able to do immeasurably more than all we ask or imagine, according to his power that is at work within us." The myth keeps young women and old women from reaching the dreams God has for them. The lie is: Cinderella felt she wasn't worthy, wasn't good enough, wasn't beautiful enough until she put on the fairy godmother gown. She couldn't see that something invaluable within herself was guiding her destiny.

Now at the risk of trying too hard to make a point with that fairy tale, I am hoping that you can see the importance of embracing the past, which includes the disappointments, the unwanted circumstances, and, yes, even the failures. These are the capstones on which God will write our story and tell it to others as we give Him permission. It is much easier to settle for portraying a fairy-tale life in not revealing who we really are. The trade-off is that it zaps us of enormous energy to keep up the facade.

Many women's ministry programs are struggling today to reach the 20- and 30-something generation. If you sit down and talk with these young women, you will hear a hunger for authenticity. They don't want games, or perfection; they want to know real-life stories that include not-so-perfect settings. They want to hear the process in wrestling with how to walk with Christ in crisis. They want to know is it OK to make mistakes, to have an emotional meltdown, to be angry, have a hard marriage or relationships that don't make sense and other hard-to-face circumstances. They desire to know that they are not alone in a world where all truth is relevant. They want to know what godly discernment looks like in order to understand real truth. That is why being transparent is so crucial. It's essential to living a life out loud with impact.

An Unlikely Leader

The story that isn't a fairy tale and helps to pull me back to reality is the story of the Samaritan woman and Jesus' amazing encounter with her at the well. It gives me great hope that God is weaving a magnificent tapestry with all the threads of my life.

The Jews hated and despised the Samaritan people. Samaria was the capital at one time of the Northern Kingdom, and when it was captured by the enemy, the Assyrians, many Jews were deported to Assyria. Foreigners were brought in to settle the land and they married the remaining Jews. So this intermarriage created hatred among the Jews toward these people, the half-breeds now named the Samaritans. The hatred was so great that traveling Jews would even take a longer route to avoid going through Samaria to get to their destination because they despised them so, to bypass the disdain of traveling through the Samaritan territory.

The story opens and we find Jesus traveling right through Samaria, going out of His way to have this encounter with this woman. When all the other Jews sought a different route, John 4:4 says, "He had to go through Samaria." This implies to me that Jesus went out of His way to speak to this woman. We land at the place in this story with Jesus sitting at the well in the heat of the day probably tired from the journey. It was very hot and here comes a lone woman to draw water from the well. Why is she coming at the heat of the day and why is she alone? It isn't hard to read between the lines when the story reveals her sordid past.

The Samaritan woman said to him, "You are a Jew and I am a Samaritan woman. How can you ask me for a drink?" (For Jews do not associate with Samaritans. Jesus answered her, "If you knew the gift of God and who it is that asks you for a drink, you would have asked him and he would have given you living water." "Sir," the woman said, "you have nothing to draw with and the well is deep. Where can you get this living water? Are you greater than our father Jacob, who gave us the well and drank from it himself, as did also his sons and his flocks and herds?" Jesus answered, "Everyone who drinks this water will be thirsty again, but whoever drinks the water I give him will never thirst. Indeed, the water I give him will become in him a spring of water welling up to eternal life." The woman said to him, "Sir, give me this water so that I won't get thirsty and have to keep coming here to draw water." He told her, "Go, call your husband and come back." "I have no husband," she replied. Jesus said to her, "You are right when you say you have no husband. The fact is, you have

had five husbands, and the man you now have is not
your husband. What you have just said is quite true"
(John 4:9–18).

Talk about a not so neat and tidy woman! The other women in the village probably despised her because of her immoral choices. She most likely felt ashamed or yet didn't want to encounter the judging stares and whispers if she were to draw her water in the cool of the day. So she chose to hide, to venture out when no one was looking. It was safer, no games to play. Yet we find Jesus engaging her in somewhat theological conversation and inviting her to receive the Living Water He offers. What was that Living Water? The chance to be forgiven, to be made new, to have a future instead of hiding from her past.

She had wandered far from God's standards because of her choices, but did that matter to Jesus? No! He looked beyond her past and saw the redemption of all the failures and the hope of glory of Christ for her future. He saw her future when everyone else was looking at her past.

The redeeming part of the story for me in the context of authenticity is how her story plays out in verses 39–42.

Many of the Samaritans from that town believed
in him because of the woman's testimony, "He told
me everything I ever did." So when the Samaritans
came to him, they urged him to stay with them, and

he stayed two days. And because of his words many more became believers. They said to the woman, "We no longer believe just because of what you said; now we have heard for ourselves, and we know that this man really is the Savior of the world."

Can you see what happened? This woman who was deemed a failure was instrumental in creating a revival in her town! She received God's Living Water and then went on to minister to others through evangelism. All because she chose to come out of hiding. She was vulnerable with Jesus, she was bold in addressing the difference between Jews and Samaritans, and revealed to Him that she had no husband when he asked her. And she received and embraced her position in Christ. When she left Jesus, she was authentic in sharing her testimony. She became the Samaritan representative for Jesus because she shed her illusions and wildly engaged God's extravagant love for her life.

Was she worthy? Was she adequate? Did she deserve what Jesus gave her? I know you know the answers to these questions. *No*, but that is what grace is all about. Grace is what propels us to be real and authentic. Grace takes away the need for our disguise and causes our hearts to sing in gratitude for what Christ has done for us. Grace covers our failures and, therefore, we can unashamedly stop worrying what others think of us and get excited about our own story and how can God lead us toward extraordinary adventures.

Taking the Hard Line

I am wondering at this point if I can push the envelope just a bit farther. Leading from an authentic place is so critical today that I believe it can make a transformational difference in your life and ministry. It isn't easy, it isn't fun, but it is rewarding as you lead others to understand the freedom that is released when we capture the beauty of living an authentic life. Jesus lived this principle out over and over again as He interacted with people.

Jesus ministered on earth as a real person. He was who He said He was, and never pretended to be any different. He was authentic in all He did and said, which is why the Pharisees hated Him so. He didn't hide behind religious robes and flaunt His godhood. He was genuine and it threatened and disgusted the religious leaders of the day.

Jesus was very serious when he called the Pharisees "whitewashed tombs, which look beautiful on the outside but on the inside, are full of dead men's bones" (Matthew 23:27 HCSB). The Pharisees were nothing but well-dressed phonies. The gospels reveal that Jesus is very clear about what God thinks about this subject. How often have we read those words about the Pharisees only to miss Jesus' point? Too often, we are just like them, slightly tweaked for the twenty-first-century. We hide our sin and failures for fear of embarrassment; we lead others astray with pretenses of "having it all together." The motivation to put up masks or veils in this area can have several origins: rejection, fear of what others will think about us, failure, learned behaviors from childhood, and the list goes on. But the truth is, when we are authentic and transparent with each other, unprecedented unity is created and compassion to love in the body. It frees us up because we all are in the same position—imperfect, flawed people who need Jesus Christ to navigate through life!

This doesn't change because we serve in a capacity of leadership. Jesus doesn't say if you are a leader, you need to present yourself as perfect to those in your sphere of influence and never show your weaknesses. He asks us to do just the opposite, lead from your place of brokenness and weakness. Paul's writing makes this clear: "My grace is sufficient for you, for my power is made perfect in weakness" (2 Corinthians 12:9 NIV). It is in our weakness that true ministry will begin to flourish with God's power. It is there that true ministry will begin to flourish. I challenge you in your next leadership meeting instead of diving into your tasks and business, lead from out of the box. Build your team with the exercise of sharing your need for God in a current area of struggle, disappointment, or frustration and have your team follow your lead. What will the results be? An authentic chapter of your life that reveals the heart of your leadership.

Can I be honest with you in stripping off another layer of a recent struggle? One of my greatest fears has been the fear of being misunderstood. The fear was realized in a storm I've had to weather recently. It went beyond what I could have even imagined and yet all along God whispered to me, "I am the God who sees. Trust Me and let Me hold that fear." It became such an escalating painful nightmare that many times I would pray, "God, I didn't sign up for this! When will You clear this up?" As the end of the storm approaches and the debris is clearing, the cloud of misunderstanding has been lifted. It felt many times as if I were stuck in a thick fog, the kind that you couldn't even see your next step.

One of the lessons for me in this was the more authentic I became, the more I risked being misunderstood and even hurt. And yet, God sorted it out in the end as I discovered and became the true person He desired me to be. In the midst of that revelation, the risk of being misunderstood and hurt was offset by the reward of helping others to have the courage to be their true selves.

You see, women, when we recognize that it is OK to feel inadequate for God's assignment, we are free to be real. After all, "It is for freedom that Christ has set us free. Stand firm then, and do not let yourselves be burdened again by a yoke of slavery" (Galatians 5:1).

Jesus, I don't want to hide any more. Pour Your light on the places that I am trying to cover up from You and others. Am I afraid, Lord, to show the real me? Help me to hang on to the promises in Your Word. Remove the yoke of being unauthentic that I might be free to lead the way for others to follow. I choose to take the risk of being misunderstood and even being hurt as I long to become more authentic. Teach me the way, Lord. I can't do it alone.

Chapter 3

Leading with Humility and Brokenness

MARY MAGDALENE

"Common looking people are the best in the world: that is the reason the Lord makes so many of them."
—ABRAHAM LINCOLN

"I long to accomplish a great and noble task, but it is my chief duty to accomplish humble tasks as though they were great and noble. The world is moved along, not only by the mighty shoves of its heroes, but also by the aggregate of the tiny pushes of each honest worker."
—HELEN KELLER

Have you ever felt stuck? Stuck in a place where you knew you couldn't stay, but weren't quite sure how you would get yourself out of for fear of embarrassment? I was stuck in the back row of an auditorium a few years ago at a leadership conference in Seattle, Washington. I had been invited to participate in a speaker's forum that would give ministry leaders an opportunity to hear new speakers that they might invite to future events. Here is where the stuck place came in for me. I was worshiping in my own little world, just God and me in the back row, when suddenly I felt a strong whack between my spiritual eyes. I sensed the words in my spirit, "Scrap your message and just tell them the truth tomorrow." I kept singing, lost in worship, and again *whack!* And the same message came, "Tell them the truth." This time I started thinking to myself while I was trying to sing, *Tell them the truth? The truth about what?* God gently whispered and challenged my motives for wanting to participate in the forum. Was it so I could showcase my gift of speaking and perform so that I would be invited to several other events? Or was it because I felt it was a privilege to exercise the gift He had given me? As I wrestled during the worship, my heart began to soften. I went back to the house where I was staying and excused myself for the evening. I went to my room and attempted to recraft the message God had given me. The original message actually ended up in the trash and God wrote on my heart with His ink the spirit of humility.

The next day as I got up to speak, I told the audience what had happened the night before and went on to talk about the importance of "learning to be little so God could be big in our lives." This was a phrase I had read early in the year in a devotional book written by Jill Briscoe. I actually made it my motto for that year, through which God would groom in me a spirit of true humility. You know the saying, "If you think you are humble, you probably aren't." I knew that I needed God in that moment. That day at the conference, I had no choice—if I wanted to invite God into my speaking, I had to learn to be little so God could be big in my life; and that meant talking about my brokenness and failures rather than my successes in order to impress. It meant stepping away from the false humility and just telling it like it was in that season of my life. In other words, it meant portraying a spirit of gratitude in the midst of failures so that the words of humility wound their way to the audience.

The Mask of Humility Versus the False Humility Syndrome

Why is it that we as women can easily say I Am Not Enough and yet at the same time act like I Am Enough? I think sometimes it is *because* we buy into the I Am Not Enough, it motivates us in our twisted thoughts to feel we have to prove ourselves. We attach a label to it that speaks through words and actions to others, can't you see? I Am Enough! It is in the performing and proving of that statement that a form of pride begins to grow in us.

The word *humility* actually means "the quality or condition of being humble." The definition speaks of humility being a prerequisite to good character or virtue. I have found more often than not we as women wear a mask of humility which often disguises a proud heart. How often have you or I heard someone say, "Oh, don't ask me. I really wouldn't be able to accomplish that"? Is that pride or humility?

There really are varying degrees of humility in the church, aren't there? There is the false humility, the manipulation to extract affirmation. Then there is the martyr humility, "I am serving because there is no one else to do it, and so God must want me to jump in." And then there is the "I am inadequate so therefore I can't be used" humility. The last one is a cousin to false humility, but it is really denying the power of God in our life to release and empower the gifts He has promised each of us. True humility has a fragrance that can't be covered up by anything else. It is so powerful that it is attractive both inside the church and out. It flourishes and reaches the hardest of hearts.

In Philippians Paul speaks of humility; this Scripture has become my cornerstone passage for leadership.

> *Is there any encouragement from belonging to Christ? Any comfort from his love? Any fellowship together in the Spirit? Are your hearts tender and compassionate? Then make me truly happy by agreeing wholeheartedly with each other, loving one another, and working together with one mind and purpose.*
>
> *Don't be selfish; don't try to impress others. Be humble, thinking of others as better than yourselves. Don't look out only for your own interests, but take an interest in others, too. You must have the same attitude that Christ Jesus had* (Philippians 2:1–5 NLT).

After pondering humility and thinking about it from Philippians 2 this is what I think it means in relation to leadership:
- We consider others better than ourselves, and I interpret that as thinking and believing the best in those we lead.

- Relinquishing control and empowering the women around me instead of trying to do everything by myself, giving the appearance that I am a super-servant.
- Having an attitude like Christ did, stepping down, instead of always trying to step up. Being brutally honest in my own assessment; that means checking my motives often.
- Being obedient, to truly listen and not rush ahead, spending time not just on our knees but on our face before God, and listening to His Spirit.
- Leading out of weaknesses rather than my human strength.

I confess to you that I still feel fairly new on this journey. In fact, I have been writing in my journal and marking the days of learning to be little so God can be big in my life. Will you join me on this journey? Just think how God could be so big in our lives that it could change our world as we influence our families, our friends, our clients, and the ministry that God has entrusted to us.

There is another aspect of humility that I want to throw in the ring for consideration. I have met a few people, and when I've listened to their stories, it seems through no fault of their own, they felt that they had to make themselves small in order to just survive, just like a new friend I met recently who grew up in an alcoholic family. Or in another scenario, someone had to minimize who they were so they wouldn't get in the way of another person's plans and dreams, all the while suppressing their own. Is this false humility? It appears from the outside to be sacrificial, but on closer inspection I am coming to grasp the truth that it could be just the plain old sin of turning over my life to someone else other than God. We all learn coping behaviors from our past; but as we respond to God and His Spirit releases us, we can be free from the learned behaviors that entrap us and keep us from flourishing.

I am still wrestling with these thoughts, but I think what I am really trying to drive home here is that true humility can't sustain being masked over by survival behaviors or our own refusal to explore the root beneath why we do what we do. Humility is recognizing the overwhelming need for God in every nook and crevice of life, even those hardened habits I've leaned on to cope when life gets overwhelming.

Fragrance of Humility

My friend Hennie is one such person. She was a captive, made to be small, but has overcome the obstacles to live in freedom in Christ. She is a tremendously happy individual who has risen from a life of hurts, disappointments, and tragedy. She has had more than her share of loss. She has walked through family deaths, cancer, bankruptcy, and widowhood. She could easily have slipped into obscurity, nursing her wounds and becoming a victim so others could serve her, but she has done just the opposite. This woman blows my mind. She has turned her losses and disappointments into windows of opportunity to encourage others.

When I first started coaching her I found it difficult to believe someone could actually respond to such tragedy in that way. The deeper we went in our coaching sessions, I discovered the secret to her responses. God's Word permeated her soul. She practiced childlike faith, believing God and cultivating a heart of gratitude. I am not sure in the end who was coaching whom. The inspiration of her journey of brokenness speaks to a fragrance of humility from her kind and gentle spirit. Hennie is having the opportunity to impact hundreds of women as she leads them in empowering themselves to live out their purpose through the ministry she leads.

Truly Simple

One chain carries a line of products touted as being truly simple organizational products designed to be used every day to simplify life. The products aren't flashy or fancy, and they are inexpensive. They work because they truly are simple. When we live a life of full-out gratitude to God, we reflect the simplicity of a life of humility. It isn't complicated; it isn't confusing; it is just pure and simple. When we are broken, a fragrance of gratitude permeates from our lives and humility is the natural result. We are in awe of how God uses us, and we are not only grateful for where we have come from, but from what God has delivered us.

Mary Magdalene was a woman who exemplified this principle. She is listed in all of the four Gospels. In Luke 8 she is listed as one of the women who traveled and supported Jesus in His ministry. It also says that Jesus had delivered her from seven demons. She was the first person to see Jesus after His resurrection. Her response when she saw Him, not recognizing Him fully, was this:

> But Mary stood outside facing the tomb, crying. As she was crying, she stooped to look into the tomb. She saw two angels in white sitting there, one at the head and one at the feet, where Jesus' body had been lying. They said to her, "Woman, why are you crying?" "Because they've taken away my Lord," she told them, "and I don't know where they've put Him." Having said this, she turned around and saw Jesus standing there, though she did not know it was Jesus. "Woman," Jesus said to her, "why are you crying? Who is it you are looking for?" Supposing He was the gardener, she replied, "Sir, if you've removed Him, tell me where you've put Him, and I will take Him away." Jesus said, "Mary." Turning around, she said to Him in Hebrew, "Rabbonni!"—which means "Teacher" (John 20:11–16 HCSB).

There are a few convincing truths that bubble to the surface when I read this passage, truths that synchronize with humility. I love the words, "They've taken away my Lord." Notice she said "my Lord." This implies to me that she had an intimate relationship with Jesus firsthand because she spent so much time with Him. He was personal to her, and she loved Him deeply. Mary served Jesus because of her gratitude for what Jesus had done for her. She didn't need to masquerade humility by acting like a victim because of her past. She didn't use her brokenness as a platform for believing the myth of I Am Not Enough and then, in turn, act on the sympathy of others to be noticed or useful. She knew she wasn't enough and didn't need to don a mask of false humility to impress others. Her brokenness was her doorway to influencing others because she knew who had rescued her from the pit of despair, discouragement, and torment. Who knows what her seven demons were? They could have been fear, depression, and a number of mental torments that the enemy sought to render her ineffective.

How often have you or I used the ploy of masquerading humility to be noticed, or to be invited to do something big for God or secure a position we have longed to have? And yes, I would be the first to confess, I've been there. I long to cultivate a heart of gratitude because of my brokenness so that humility just naturally oozes from my life to others, don't you?

Lord Jesus, help me to learn to be little so You can be big in my life. I want to be like Mary and call You "my Lord." Smooth the ragged edges of my life that need to simplify in order to live a life of humility. Permeate my soul with thoughts and words of gratitude so that I might leave a fragrance of humility wherever I go.

IT'S NOT THE RIGHT TIME

Myth 2

Chapter 4

Leading with Courage

ESTHER

"If you lose hope, somehow you lose the vitality that keeps
life moving, you lose that courage to be, that quality that
helps you go on in spite of it all.
And so today I still have a dream."
—Martin Luther King Jr.

A favorite childhood memory is sitting with my sister in our pajamas curled up with our blankets while watching one of our favorite characters in the classic movie *The Wizard of Oz*. The Cowardly Lion was faced with the greatest challenge of his life in the forest he had lived in comfortably for so long. By his own confession, he was a great coward and this was his moment to shine. He was asked by his traveling companions, the Tin Man and Scarecrow, to risk life and limb to rescue Dorothy and her dog, Toto, who had been captured by the awful Wicked Witch of the West. He told them sheepishly but with a burst of courage, "All right, I'd go in there for Dorothy. Wicked witch or no wicked witch, guards or no guards, I'll tear them apart. I may not come out alive, but I'm going in there. There's only one thing I want you fellows to do." His friends replied, "What's that?" To which the Lion said, "Talk me out of it."

Can you relate? Once you have had a burst of courage to do the impossible, have you asked God or your friends to talk you out of it? When is the proper time to look fear in the face as a leader, to accomplish what God might be asking? Is it waiting until everything falls into place? Is it shouting from the forest and engaging others to do the job for you? How do we know when and where to move ahead?

Eleanor Roosevelt once said, "You gain strength, courage, and confidence by every experience in which you really stop to look fear in the face. You are able to say to yourself, 'I have lived through this horror. I can take the next thing that comes along.' You must do the thing you think you cannot do."

I would like to add that you *must do* the thing that you *know* you cannot do apart from God's amazing strength. That is the prerequisite to doing what you know you can't possibly do, which is real courage. The Bible is full of examples of cowards who looked fear in the face and acted with God-infused courage. I have a feeling if we wait for courage, it will never come. But as the Cowardly Lion in *The Wizard of Oz* discovered, he did have courage when he faced his fear.

When Is the Right Time?

IT's Not the Right Time, our second myth that we need to shatter, is to step up to the task to which God may be calling you or me. Using the excuse, It's Not the Right Time, when God whispers a mission in your spiritual ear, we can easily masquerade and join the Cowardly Women's Club (a.k.a. CWC). It is much easier to stay in the forest where we know our surroundings and our familiar paths. It is a much greater risk to actually step foot outside of the forest that we have made our life. Guess what pushed the Cowardly Lion to step out of his comfort zone? His friend Dorothy's dilemma. It allowed him to look fear in the face, to risk his own comfort for the sake of friendship, to save someone he cared about.

Somehow when we take up a cause greater than ourselves, our own cowardice and fears diminish. It's like we can feel ourselves stand up taller and reach higher because we know that the safety and well-being of others are involved. If you are a mom, you know you would risk everything to keep your children safe if they were in harm's way. When God instills a dream, a mission, a cause in your heart, then He gives you the tools to look past the obstacles that might keep you in the CWC. He whispers, "Trust Me, I am your confidence, your rock, I will equip you for this journey."

God's Timing the First Time

Jocelyn Jelsma is a mother of four children ranging in age from 14 to 5 years old. She and her husband served in the Philippines for a year, using the skills they had acquired in midwifery and primary health care to love the poorest of the poor. Jocelyn and her husband came back to their home in Canada with their hearts wrecked forever by what they had experienced in loving those less fortunate. That year of ministry was the beginning of God dropping a dream in her heart, a dream to reach out to women who by being empowered with simple education could reduce infant mortality and keep their children and their families healthier.

At first they settled back into their normal routine and wondered if God might have an assignment for them in the future when their family was older. They had a young family and it seemed impossible to think that a tribe of six could manage such a mission. In the meantime, the church they were attending had been praying about starting a medical clinic in Rwanda, where the infant mortality rate is high. What seemed impossible both for the Jelsmas and the church became a reality in less than two years. In October 2008 this young family journeyed 36 hours to their new home in Kigali, Rwanda. I remember saying to Jocelyn that I thought she was the bravest woman I knew to venture to such a place where there were so many unknowns. She told me she was grappling with a number of fears. Her younger children were small; the risk of disease and sickness was a great possibility with limited quality care in the region.

Before she and her family left, we sat around with a few girl-friends and shared all kinds of funny stories about spiders, bugs, rats, the likes of which they knew they would encounter. She voiced her fears, but with quiet confidence, knowing that this was God's mission for their lives. She was prepared not for the unknown, but for God gearing her up to face her fears one step at a time. As we saw them off at the airport, the reality of what they were about to do became concrete. Yes, Jocelyn was afraid, and yes, she probably wished she could stay in her comfortable surroundings and raise her children in a familiar routine. In spite of her tearful good-bye, this was a woman who knew by God's strength she was called to be a mother to other mothers and lead them to health and wellness both physically and spiritually. Jocelyn is one of my heroes and mentors in responding to God's timing with courage in spite of being afraid.

You see, to wait on what *we* feel the right timing is for an assignment really isn't biblical truth in what we might understand about facing our fears. God asks us sometimes to just jump and trust Him. In my experience I have rarely found an individual who has not been afraid at some point to take on the assignment God is asking. Often it does feel overwhelming and we may have several obstacles to conquer. We are tempted to give up too easily and even assess, "This might not be God's will." We quit. Adversity and determination are the making of a heart of courage. I will be the first to confess that fear has overwhelmed me. I have come to the conclusion that if I wait to feel courageous, I will be waiting indefinitely. Rather I am learning that sometimes you just have to take that first step even in the midst of being afraid. Walking with God, confidently keeping our eye on the goal, is paramount to the success of the mission. Listen to what Paul says,

"That is why we never give up. Though our bodies are dying, our spirits are being renewed every day. For our present troubles are small and won't last very long. Yet

> they produce for us a glory that vastly outweighs them
> and will last forever! So we don't look at the troubles
> we can see now; rather, we fix our gaze on things that
> cannot be seen. For the things we see now will soon be
> gone, but the things we cannot see will last forever"
> (2 Corinthians 4:16–18 NLT).

Leading with courage. Afraid Esther is a favorite Bible story among women. Her brave resolve in revealing the wicked plot of Haman to destroy the Jews places her in the courage hall of fame. She risked her own life to save her people by barging into the throne room unannounced, which even for the queen meant certain death. She faced her fears, but because she was truly human, ran through her own set of uncertainties in calculating the risks. This account from the Bible implies that she did indeed have questions and fears. Yet she felt safe behind the palace walls with the secret of her heritage hidden beneath her queenly crown.

> *Mordecai told [the messenger] to reply to Esther,*
> *"Don't think that you will escape the fate of all the*
> *Jews because you are in the king's palace. If you keep*
> *silent at this time, liberation and deliverance will*
> *come to the Jewish people from another place, but you*
> *and your father's house will be destroyed. Who knows,*
> *perhaps you have come to your royal position for such*
> *a time as this." Esther sent this reply to Mordecai: "Go*
> *and assemble all the Jews who can be found in Susa*
> *and fast for me. Don't eat or drink for three days, day*

or night. I and my female servants will also fast in the same way. After that, I will go to the king even if it is against the law. If I perish, I perish" (Esther 4:13–18 HCSB).

Contrast the two phrases: first, the myth of It's Not the Right Time, and second "for such a time as this"? Maybe we should ask when hearing God's quiet nudge of an assignment, "Is what You are asking, God, for such a time as this?"

Here is an assignment for you (if you choose to accept it). It is in three parts. If you are sensing at this moment that God is calling you to a mission outside of yourself that seems utterly impossible and has you totally scared spitless, don't say no quickly, dismissing it as a crazy notion, but follow these steps:

1. Why not pray this phrase as a question, "For such a time as this, God?"
2. Fast and pray as Esther did. Allow God to speak to you to give you the next step of action.
3. Write down all the obstacles you can possibly think of at the moment. Name your fears and what-ifs (for example, time, money, relationships, etc.), then present it as an impossibility offering to God, letting Him know that this is where you are afraid. In other words, girlfriend, name your fears!

4. Take the first step! And if you have to, step out while you are afraid.

The Way Out to Lead with Courage

Robert Frost said, "The best way out is always through." Are you looking for a way out or a way through to reach what you know God has for you? It always stumps me to think how our scope is so limited in comparison to what God says about who we are and what His designed purpose is for you and me. He really and truly believes in us, yet when He even remotely suggests a mission uniquely handcrafted for us, how quickly we run back to the safety of the forest and hang out with the other cowardly lions. It is seemingly safer to dream and imagine from the confines of our comfortable state of what we have created than to venture into the unknown. The Cowardly Lion in the end received his medal of courage from the Wizard, not because he became more courageous, but I think because he dared to step out of the forest and face his fears.

That, my friends, is the only way out to lead with courage. First, we take action to be courageous enough to address our fears, and second, we act with courage to take the first step. Does that sound like obedience to you?

Esther, Deborah, Gideon, Moses, Sarah, David, Ruth, Peter, Paul, and a pack of others in the Bible are real people who led with courage despite hardships and monumental obstacles. We all have one thing in common, a fearless King who gives us this promise: "Don't be afraid, for I am with you. Don't be discouraged, for I am your God. I will strengthen you and help you. I will hold you up with my victorious right hand" (Isaiah 41:10 NLT).

Lord Jesus, thank You for the visual of holding us up with Your right hand. Thank You for reminding me that You are always with me; and with You next to me leading the way, I can face my fears. Help me to trust that You are orchestrating my life for this very moment. I can't see the big picture, but You are the one who knows every detail. I rest and draw my strength from You. Turn my fear into courage, God, courage to trust You; courage to walk by faith, courage to believe the impossible is possible with You.

Chapter 5

Leading Through Change

SARAH

"Become a student of change.
It is the only thing that will remain constant."
—ANTHONY D'ANGELO

"Sarai, it's time to go," her husband called from the front entrance. "I know, I am coming," she said as her fingers lingered over a favored vase on an inlaid table. "Everyone is waiting, Sarai, please hurry," the voice of her husband echoed in the front courtyard through the entrance of their home which they had lived for so long. How could I have let this happen, why did I agree to follow this man to an unknown place? She had never seen her husband, Abram, so enthralled and passionate about anything in several years. This new God, *Yahweh,* had spoken to her husband directly giving him a promise to make him into a great nation. He spoke with such intensity as he told me the whole story, I didn't know what to believe at first. Anyone who is familiar with Abram knows that once he gets an idea into his head, there is no stopping him. What was I to do, but go along with him? At this point his mind was made up. He promised me adventure and said it was about time we had a change of scenery, or so he said. It was hard enough to leave the first time when we ventured out from Ur. And now since Terah's death, Abram seemed bent on leaving Haran. Was he being rational or was this his grief over the loss of his father speaking?

Sarai had just begun to feel settled with friends to ease away the loneliness of not being able to have a child. And now this, pack up and leave everything again to go off to a desolate place no one has ever heard of? She was getting too old for these kinds of adventures, she thought to herself. I can see Sarai in my mind. As Sarai walked through her lovely home one more time, her eyes falling on the familiar, she knew they would never be back. This was final. Even though she wasn't sure what lay ahead, she had no choice but to embrace the change that was about to descend.

Sound familiar? I say Sarai was quite a woman to be able to move through the change that life was throwing at her—or rather changes her husband was leading her through. Sarai had some tough choices to make, and I am sure she wrestled with feelings and emotions as she sought to make sense of the upheaval of her comfortable life. When most of us are ready to retire at age 65 and settle in for our golden years, Abram was dragging Sarai around the country on a wild adventure.

If you read between the lines of the story in Genesis, Sarai was an ordinary woman who was tested to the limit. Her faith was challenged, and to top it off she was challenged physically in her old age when God revealed to her that she was indeed finally going to have a son, the son of their destiny that would be the seed of the nations. When I read about her life, I see a woman who encountered over-the-top changes to which she responded with a myriad of human emotions. The bottom line is she did get through all of the changes, maybe not perfectly, but she made it through. Sarai was probably not much unlike you or me. She had tangled emotions marked with uncertainty and doubts.

I am very fond of this story in Genesis. I can see Sarai as someone just like myself, entirely human from the whole spectrum. One doesn't have to read too far into the story to relate to what could have been an onslaught of emotions as she contended with the obstacles ranging from being masqueraded as Abram's sister to taking charge of producing the promise God had given. Some of these choices, which were of her own choosing—others her husband's—didn't always have favorable outcomes. In the end, she is heralded as a woman in Hebrews 11:11 who trusted God and found Him faithful as promised.

Just when we start to get a bit comfortable, life seems to send us a wind of change. I am not sure what God is thinking when He allows it, but one thing I am learning these past few years is that change is inevitable. So I am better off to just resign myself to lean in rather than fight the changes. As we follow the journey of Sarai in the Book of Genesis, we see that her life really became days, months, and years filled with uncertainty and change. There didn't seem to be an end—but there was. The promise that came in their son Isaac was the fulfillment of God's dream not only for her and her husband but for the nation of Israel as well.

The Wind of Change

We can't see the wind, but we can feel it. We can't even see it coming. Sometimes we can hear it coming in the distance; usually that is an indication of a rather immense storm that is about to descend.

A few summers ago, I couldn't see the wind of change that was coming, but I heard it rustle in the distance. Even the rustling caught me off guard. Our youngest son, Jason, decided he wanted to move into a condo with three other guys while he attended school just 45 minutes away. In addition to his moving out, he informed Kevin and me of his intention to marry this amazing girl he had been bringing home week in and week out. I had told him at his brother's wedding, which happened in a blink of an eye, that I needed at least three years to recover before I could even think about him leaving us for good. But he was resolute.

You see, I am discovering that I don't like change very much. In fact, this concept has been a real eye-opener for me that I am getting older and change is happening more rapidly than expected. I want to tell you that I haven't handled it as well as I wanted to. But I haven't handled it very well, and I have been succumbing to all sorts of lies and thoughts from the enemy.

I have dwelt on the notion that my 30-year job as a mom is over and now who am I? Who needs me? I don't know how to cook for two—I only know how to cook for football teams of boys and men. I have asked myself several questions. During that season, I found myself wallowing in self-absorption and becoming discontent with just about everything, having a hard time focusing on a task or a goal, and, believe me, I had lots to do. People were depending on me to continue leading in the areas God had called me to lead.

I could see it happening, and yet I felt so mixed up and befuddled. I used to literally laugh at women in this situation. I would think, *What are they so sad about? I will be lighting fireworks and celebrating!* Now I understand why those women were sad. Yes, I am so blessed to see my boys flourishing each in their own way, but it feels like a terrible thing not to be needed anymore in the same ways. I could have hundreds of women say they need me, but it doesn't hold a candle to being needed by my boys.

Change in life can be disconcerting, but the winds of change are inevitable. We can't stop it, but we can take the perspective that how we respond to the changes and transitions in life determines how well we will do. So you know what I did?

I was up late reading a book to help me on the journey when I stopped and thought, *This is ridiculous.* I had a good cry and fell on my knees before the Lord, asking Him to help me not be obsessed over these changes, and to help me transition through them with His love and strength. I told God exactly how I felt about everything. And you know what? He responded as He always does, with love and compassion. I got out my pen and paper and started listing all the things I needed to get in order. I needed to start doing something for someone else and quit feeling sorry for myself and get focused. God had laid out some incredible things for me and I couldn't see that past the change

I was holding on to. Now that's not to say I didn't have to deal with a lot of emotions. I was just more aware and able to grieve and move forward in a more positive way. Did I say it was easy? Not really, but change is complicated and that's OK as long as I invite God to be on the journey.

Change is all about adjusting, transitioning, and transforming. When we order up our own change of correcting a bad habit or refocusing in an area of our leadership development, somehow it seems OK. The true test of how we weather change in our lives comes when it hits us unexpectedly like a rush of unexpected wind.

One of the toughest areas in weathering change is how it affects my personal leadership of others. My gut reaction is to just hide it, muddle through, and hope that nobody notices I am struggling. Or even feeling like I should step down until I can get my act together and wait for conditions that merit right timing. I am learning that this isn't necessarily the best way to be an effective leader. The women I lead know me and have watched me respond to all kinds of circumstances. The greatest gift I can give them is to help them enter into my change as much as possible and as much as is appropriate. We are a team, and when one of us is struggling, it affects us all and in turn makes us stronger as a core unit flourishing for a common purpose. Our team in that season had seen everything from children getting married, an unwed pregnancy, cancer treatment, job changes, to smaller life changes. These and other seasons are real changes, and frankly they do take us by surprise. But they are the hiccups in life that determine our character as we navigate through the unexpected curves that life seems to throw at us.

Unexpected and unwelcome change creates an opportunity to adjust our attitude. It gives us the privilege of reexamining just exactly what we are doing and how to make a shift if needed. Nothing is wasted, ever. God knows exactly what He is doing every single minute of your life. Yet, often my response when faced with change is not embracing it as an opportunity. Instead I buy into the myth of IT'S NOT THE RIGHT TIME. I tell God, "Hey, You got it wrong, not now, not here, not ever, please!" I am so glad that God doesn't take me too seriously when I am ranting and raving in my initial reactions. He is so patient, and so good, and oh so faithful.

What helps me to adjust to the change and respond positively to the opportunity God is giving me is found in Romans 12:2 (NLT): "Don't copy the behavior and customs of this world, but let God transform you into a new person by changing the way you think. Then you will learn to know God's will for you, which is good and pleasing and perfect." The word *transform* in this passage is *metamorphoo* in Greek. It is the root word for *metamorphosis*, which means "to change into another form."

In other words, don't whine, complain, moan, and groan when change arrives. Instead we should follow Paul's instructions by letting God change the way we think. That is the key—to change the way we think about the change. I am not saying you can't have a moment with negative emotions. That's actually healthy. It's just not God's plan to camp there and cement those emotions in your heart.

I don't have to remind you that what you are is a result of what you think, not what you feel. What you think is a result of how you behave. How you behave is a result of your character. How your character is revealed is how you react to change. How you change is a result of how you think. So what we need to do is change our thinking. I have struggled with this and agonized over the will to change my thoughts. But it is clear, that is the pathway to transformation.

When I was a kid I was fascinated with caterpillars. I collected them. I watched them closely, waiting for their glorious transformation. I wasn't very patient. I expected to see the whole process overnight, I think. When that little caterpillar that I had watched in the cocoon (which seemed like forever) emerged and left an empty cocoon, I watched for the butterfly. Of course, I never actually found the actual butterfly that belonged to the cocoon, but I liked to think I did.

Our transformation is a process, just like a caterpillar's change to a butterfly. It doesn't happen overnight, but the idea is that by changing our thinking it leads us to move into the change that God desires. I don't know about you, but I don't want to stay a caterpillar. I want to be a butterfly. The process is crucial, but more importantly allowing God to lead me through the change will result in godly transformation.

What comes out of the transforming process as we let God in on it produces a magnificent gem in our character development. There are no ifs, ands, or buts about it; God gives us a promise that when we are transformed, we will be able to discern the next steps in our lives. Isn't that what happens when change throws us a curve, it can momentarily paralyze our plans and agendas? I think God sees it as an opportunity for us to readjust to his plan. When change hits the first thing we tend to address is "What do I do now?" It throws us off course momentarily. The answer lies in this concise yet powerful verse of Scripture. Here are some steps we can take:

1. Don't listen to and buy into our culture and join the whiner's club.

2. See the unexpected change as an opportunity to change your thinking about what is happening.

3. Look ahead for the direction God wants to reveal to you as your thinking adjusts.

We can learn from Sarah's life when the promise God had given her seemed to fade. She gave up and didn't adjust her thinking by focusing on God's original promise to her. She bought into her culture and therefore made a huge detour in her faith by encouraging her husband to give her a son through her servant Hagar. You can bet this wasn't God's ultimate plan for her life, but God uses even our detours to make a difference.

Carol Kent, in her book *A New Kind of Normal*, states how her life went from one extreme to another overnight. Reading the tragic story of how her only son ended up in maximum security prison, serving a life sentence for murder, is sobering. Yet her journey through that change is inspiring.

I had the privilege of meeting Carol at a conference a few years ago where we were both speaking. What I saw was a woman who had allowed God to change her thinking about this drastic transition in her life. It has become a part of her story and her next level of ministry. It hasn't been easy for her. She and her husband live with the life-altering change day after day. As she says in her book, "This is my new kind of normal."

Jesus, help me to not be a whiner and complainer when change comes, especially unexpectedly. Help me to trust You and not my feelings. Change my thoughts, Lord. It will help me in the process of trusting You.

GOD CAN'T USE ME BECAUSE OF MY PAST

Myth 3

Chapter 6

Leading with Perspective

HAGAR

"If you have made mistakes, there is always another chance for you.
You may have a fresh start any moment you choose, for this thing
we call 'failure' is not the falling down, but the staying down."
—MARY PICKFORD

"My reputation grows with every failure."
—GEORGE BERNARD SHAW

Walking on the beach in Hawaii one summer, I was inspired to start a collection of sea glass. A friend of ours who had been collecting sea glass for several years led me down the beach and showed me the fine art of detecting sea glass hidden in the sand. We must have walked along the shoreline for over an hour. I found 10 or 15 pieces of glass that had been weathered and tumbled by the sand and sea.

Looking for sea glass is not for the person on a tight schedule. Quickly scanning the beachfront will not help you find these treasures. It takes time.

There are four different colors of sea glass—shades of amber, white, blue, and green. Other colors may be found, but are rare. One of the highlights of our vacation was searching for these lovely colors, which forced me to slow down and look with a different perspective at the beauty of the Hawaiian beaches.

Sea glass comes from ordinary bottles—everyday glass objects, such as soda bottles, that never make it to the trash bin. What amazes me is that a finished piece of intricately polished sea glass was once part of a broken, cast-off bottle. Over a period of years the ocean sifts the glass. It is crushed on the rocks into multiple pieces as waves pound endlessly on the shore. The labels are washed off, and over time the sharp pieces of glass become polished by the sand and saltwater. What emerges on the beach and becomes a treasure is a smooth, unusually shaped piece of colorful glass that connoisseurs spend hours searching for to add to their collection.

I couldn't help but think that our lives are much like those bottles that become sea glass; broken, shattered, having labels attached to us that seek to define us and keep us from being all that God wants us to be. We are convinced that God couldn't possibly create something beautiful from our past, our mistakes, or even our traumas. We relinquish our faith that God can transform us. We accept life is riddled with failure, and for some, the reminder of this scars us for life.

I can't tell you how often I have seen women paralyzed from moving forward because they believed the myth of God Can't Use Me Because of My Past. I have seen women of all ages settle for less than God intended, because they believe the lie that God couldn't possibly turn their broken and shattered lives into a beautiful treasure of sea glass.

A LEADER WITH A DIVERSE PERSPECTIVE

Nancy Alcorn is a visionary leader with the perspective of seeing young women aged 13–28 who feel they are castoffs as potentials for a miracle. Here is her incredible story of bringing hope to these young women.

 It was during and after college that Nancy Alcorn, a native Tennessean, spent eight years working for the state of Tennessee at a correctional facility for juvenile delinquent girls and investigating child abuse cases. Working for the state on a daily basis gave her direct encounters with the secular programs that were not producing permanent results that exemplified changed lives. Nancy saw many of the girls pass the age of 18 and end up in the women's prison system because they never got the real help they needed. After working for the state and recognizing that true transformation would never come as the result of any government system, she was appointed director of women for Nashville Teen Challenge where she worked for two years. Through her experience, she began to realize that only Jesus could bring restoration into the lives of the girls who were desperately hurting and searching for something to fill the void they felt in their hearts. As her spirit was stirred and her passion ignited, Nancy knew that God was revealing a destiny that would result in her stepping out to help these hurting women.

In January 1983, determined to establish a program to truly transform lives, Nancy moved to Monroe, Louisiana, to start Mercy Ministries of America. As she began to lay the groundwork for the establishment of the ministry, she knew that there were three principles to which she must always remain faithful: (1) do not take any state or federal funding that may limit the freedom to teach Christian principles; (2) accept girls free of charge; and (3) always give at least 10 percent of all Mercy Ministries' donations to other organizations and ministries.

Several years and many changed lives later, Mercy Ministries has established locations in Monroe, Louisiana; Nashville, Tennessee; St. Louis, Missouri; and in the Sacramento, California, area. The organization has grown beyond the borders of the United States, including affiliates in the United Kingdom, Canada, and New Zealand. In addition, plans are under way for more sites in America as well as internationally.

According to Nancy, "It is our belief that if we provide places at no charge where girls can come and

receive new life through Jesus Christ, as well as professional training in other areas, their lives will never
be the same!"

I am moved by Nancy's mission to release wholeness in these
shattered young girls. I have had the privilege of seeing her in
action and she is a formidable woman with phenomenal faith.

Hagar: An Unlikely Perspective

In the backside of the desert a young woman pregnant, scared,
and alone with no hope for the future met, in her own words,
"the God Who Sees." She had run away from her mistress Sarai
(later known as Sarah) who had spurned and mistreated her
because she had gotten pregnant through her master Abram
(later known as Abraham). I can only imagine how confused
Hagar must have felt. Sarai had willing given Hagar to Abram
to intervene and hurry up the promise of a son God had given
the couple years earlier. When the timing didn't happen quickly
enough for Sarai, she decided to help God out by following the
ancient custom of a barren woman being able to bear a child
through a slave. So now Sarai had what she wanted, but it was
proving to be too much emotional wrenching for her heart. It
was poking at the wound of not being able to conceive, and
Hagar became the target of her wounds.

Hagar, confused and lost, finds herself face-to-face with
God in the wilderness.

An angel of GOD found her beside a spring in the desert; it was the spring on the road to Shur. He said, "Hagar, maid of Sarai, what are you doing here?" She said, "I'm running away from Sarai my mistress." The angel of GOD said, "Go back to your mistress. Put up with her abuse." He continued, "I'm going to give you a big family, children past counting.

From this pregnancy, you'll get a son: Name him Ishmael;

for GOD heard you, GOD answered you.

He'll be a bucking bronco of a man,

a real fighter, fighting and being fought,

Always stirring up trouble,

always at odds with his family."

She answered GOD by name, praying to the God who spoke to her, "You're the God who sees me!" "Yes! He saw me; and then I saw him!" (Genesis 16:7–13 *The Message*).

Don't you love when God states the obvious? He asks her first, "What are you doing here?" Whatever mess we find ourselves in, a mistake, a failure, or a wound at someone else's hand, God desires to know what is in our heart. Then and only then can He help us to see the situation from His perspective. She must have thought, *What was God thinking telling me to go back and endure the mistreatment?* As only God can, He gave her the next step with a promise to embrace. He knew that she would need that promise to endure the coming days and months.

A bit of a disclaimer here, just so you don't misunderstand the truth of this story. I am quite sure that God knew in sending her back that she would be protected for the fulfillment of His promise to her. I am not advocating sending anyone back into an abusive situation where they are in serious physical harm. I believe that God wouldn't have sent Hagar back if she would have been severely mistreated and physically in danger. He promised her a son and a brighter future, and God gave her the ability to trust Him in returning to her mistress.

Hagar was able to believe in her future because her perspective changed. God not only heard her desperate cries, but also gave her a promise for the future, a glimpse of what was going to happen.

Isn't that what we all need, someone to hear our misery and to infuse us with hope? When that happens, it helps us gain perspective; more importantly it helps us to be open to seeing our circumstances from God's perspective.

Too often we dismiss hope in our lives by allowing ourselves to be defined by our past. Whether it is mistakes we have made or the failure of others, it is too easy to lose perspective. It comes to settle in deep in our spirit, to make and set up camp threatening to take over permanently. The temptation is to just stay in the pit and feel sorry for ourselves.

I want to say two things here. First, we are not defined by our past in any way. God uses the brokenness of our past to shape our future. The finest leaders I know or have read about in history are those who have a past that included broken and sordid, failures, struggles, and adversities that converged upon their lives either suddenly or slowly. It seems that the greater the assignment, the deeper the school of pain. This reality is fresh for me because of a recent storm I mentioned earlier that lasted longer than I signed up for. Every time I thought it was over another wave swept over, bringing me to crash against the rocks without hope of being at the end.

Finally, at this writing, I can see the storm clearing. I am still unpacking the whirlwind of change; without giving all the details, let's just call what happened a perfect storm, a tsunami combined with a hurricane that threatened to destroy and take me out. Just like the sea glass roughed up by the sand and tumbling in the waves, many times in this season I felt lost and disillusioned. Even in the swirling of the sand blinding me in the surf, I am learning to accept pain as my friend rather than an enemy. I have discovered that there is purpose in pain. There may not be clarity in the pain, but I choose to believe that God is still God. He sits on the throne of heaven underscoring every single detail of my life. It is the pain of failure, the pain of a mistake, or the pain of suffering at someone else's hand that takes me to the next level of being the person that God has destined me to be. The lessons of pain from my past free me to breathe hope to others. It grants me the tremendous privilege to empower another tired, desperate soul toward seeing a glimpse of God's perspective on what they are experiencing.

Second, the privilege of leadership affords me to be on the lookout for other broken women who have grappled with their own past, recognizing it is what gives them the ability to accomplish the mission God has given to them. These are the women that I want to hang out with and call my companions. I am weary of the conundrum of achieving perfection as a person and as a leader. Living with pain as my friend has granted me the immense joy of knowing that because of my past I can be free to impact others beyond what I would even imagine. It is the common thread that shouts to other women, "She is like me! A rough piece of broken glass and I know that I am not alone."

I wish we could sit down face-to-face so I could stare into your eyes and say to you, "Please don't believe the lie that God can't use you because of your past!" He can't give you your future if He doesn't have your past. You are the only person who can give it back to Him as a gift so He can burnish it in the sea of His love to produce a priceless piece of sea glass. The sharp edges He rubs away with the gentle scouring of His endless love. He shapes the glass, washes away the labels, and moves it over and through the waves brushing against the sand countless times until He has it in the exact place to be discovered and used for His glory.

Would you believe that there is actually an organization for serious sea glass collectors? It is called the North American Sea Glass Association. They have strong guidelines for those who claim to be hobbyists of sea glass. There are numerous pictures on their Web site of how not to be defrauded if you are buying sea glass, how to distinguish the difference between those pieces put through a rock tumbler and those unique pieces actually churned by the sea. If you look closely, it is easy to detect the difference in the beauty of the true sea glass.

A life that has been tumbled in a rock tumbler is a life that tries to control the circumstances; it produces an inauthentic piece of sea glass. It isn't nearly as attractive as a life roughed up by grains of sand and the crashing against the rocks. A life set free to be polished by the hands of the Master has a greater depth and translucence of beauty.

I am not sure about your circumstances or mind-set while you are reading this book, but let me leave you with a promise from Isaiah 43:18–19 (HCSB). As God has made a way in the wilderness for a woman like Hagar, He can make a way for you and me.

Do not remember the past events; pay no attention to things of old. Look, I am about to do something new; even now it is coming. Do you not see it? Indeed, I will make a way in the wilderness, rivers in the desert.

Jesus, so often I get trapped by my past. It is like an old tape playing over and over again trying to derail my ability to see you in the desert. Lord Jesus, I give You my past, everything that is an obstacle for me to embrace the future You have for me. Thank You that see You my past as an opportunity and not as a roadblock. I give it to You now as a gift for You to tumble and polish for the future. Lord, change my perspective; let me see my life through Your eyes of love, healing, and transformation.

Chapter 7

Leading with Unresolved Issues

JEZEBEL

*"We learn wisdom from failure much more than from
success. We often discover what will do, by finding out
what will not do; and probably he who never made a
mistake never made a discovery."*
—SAMUEL SMILES

It was opening night of our Christmas Dessert Theatre
production. Our team had worked diligently for several
months for this very night. Hundreds of people from our
community would be streaming in the doors momentarily,
some for the first time, others for their once-a-year patronage in
the name of religion.

I was walking through the entrance finishing up the last
details when in walked one of my stage managers, Rochelle.
She greeted me excitedly; she took her role very seriously. Her
mantra was to be "a light shining in the dark." You see, she used
her flashlight backstage during the performance giving direction
and helping the cast on and off the stage. Her mantra was a

reminder of what our purpose was for our production and she frequently cheerfully reminded us as we walked onto the stage. She was rushing to resume her post when I curtly reminded her that she had made a mistake and hadn't come through the right entrance. I had instructed the cast and crew to come through the back door to minimize the traffic and keep things looking fresh for our guests. As soon as the words fell out of my mouth, I saw her face fall in dismay. I quickly tried to make light of it, saying it really didn't matter. She was very gracious and went on her way to get to her post on time. Immediately, I chastised myself. "How could I? What's wrong with me?"

It was during that season in my early leadership that incidents like that happened often. No matter how hard I tried, it seemed I failed miserably over and over again. A revelation started to take place. I realized that underneath the appearance of a strong capable leader was a small, seismic volcano bubbling. The greater the stress and pressure during that season, the more it seemed to occur. It was like a vaporous poison was seeping out from my boiling heart.

I decided to talk about it with a friend (the one who works as a professional counselor). As we dialogued over my situation, I slowly came to realize that I was emotionally handicapped. In other words, when pain or disappointment hit my heart, I had built a protective wall over it. I lived denying the pain and its consequential impact. As a result over time, the "emotional stuff" behind the wall became too much to contain and it started leaking out in negative ways. I made a commitment to start to tear down the walls and deal with the junk because it was starting to stink up my life and impact those closest to me. Mixed in with performance issues were feelings of pride and anger that I couldn't just put a Band-Aid® on and get over. I needed to do some serious excavating of my heart to uncover the root of what was driving me with these unhealthy behaviors.

With the help of my good friend and a program at our church, I determined to uncover the mystery of why I had built the wall in the first place. I remember telling everyone I was going to participate for the three months and be done—what a joke! Imagine telling your doctor how long it will take to recover from serious surgery. That's how ridiculous that statement was. I was in fact telling God how long He could work to take down the wall, empty the trash, and make my heart squeaky clean.

I don't remember exactly how long it took to actually tear down the wall completely. In some ways I feel I am still in the process of removing the remainder of the rubble because at times I am tempted to pick up the spade and build a new section of wall over my heart when I get hurt.

I have since learned that there are rhythms and movements of growth within my leadership calling. When God wants to take me to greater depths, He forces the issues in my life to be purged. My soul has to continue to be nurtured to maintain the level of leadership God has directed me in. That means I have to be aware of how I interact in my relationships and with those that I lead. I have come to practice what I like to call emotional soul-talk to keep my heart in check.

Peter Scazzero, in his very profound book *Emotionally Healthy Spirituality*, stresses the importance of understanding your level of emotional health. I think it is paramount as leaders to not only know this about yourself but also to understand how it relates to your effectiveness as a leader. The deception is that we tend to think when our ministry is falling apart and we, too, are falling apart, that is the time to have a checkup. That is not necessarily the truth. Often it is when we are at the height of success and are getting ready to move to another level that our soul hasn't been nurtured enough and hasn't caught up with our current level of leadership. This is a critical time and many men and women either capsize or grow through their season of revelation.

Do we wait for the seeping of negative thoughts and actions to pay attention to our heart? No, I believe we are to keep a keen sense of listening and learning about the movements within our hearts.

Learning to Breathe

Breathing is an automatic response that we rarely think about. Each breath is a reminder that we are alive. Each breath is a sign that life moves forward whether we will it or not. There is pain so tumultuous at times that it feels as though we can barely take a breath.

It is usually at those times that we have trouble taking the next step; it is all we can do to survive. It is during that time God gets our attention. As C. S. Lewis has said: "Pain is God's megaphone to the World." God wants to speak to us to reveal Himself to us. As a leader this is so very critical! Leading with unresolved pain, issues, and circumstances is a formula for stunting our leadership. Inhaling the pain deep into our hearts and allowing it to fill our spiritual lungs allows God to do His best work. It is in the exhalation that the hurt, wound, and problems get released. But when we hold our breath, so to speak, it only gives opportunity for us to not be able to function properly. We can pass out!

JEZEBEL: A WOMAN WITH UNRESOLVED ISSUES

Have you ever heard of anyone naming his or her child Jezebel? Not likely. She is known as one of the most infamous, evil, wicked queens in biblical history. She was a strong woman of character (evil character) devoted solely to the idol Baal. She made it her passion in life to convert her subjects and to influence them toward Baal worship. God had enough and sent Elijah the prophet to challenge her worship of Baal and Asherah. She hunted down the last of the prophets of Israel and Judah and had them slaughtered, minus 100 prophets that were hidden by Obadiah. There was a big showdown on Mount Carmel with the prophets of Baal and Elijah of whose God is bigger than my God, and, of course, as I like to think of it, Almighty God received the Academy Award for Best Picture. This infuriated Jezebel and she sought to have Elijah killed. God protected Elijah, and eventually Queen Jezebel and her evil counterpart King Ahab came to their doom by the judgment of God.

Jezebel's story reveals her thirst for power and control. Nothing could stop her in her tantrum rage to have her own way. There was no peaceful negotiating; it was all her way or the highway. Her life speaks to me of a woman who didn't know her own heart. She was relentless in her demands that her subjects to follow Baal, destroying all in her path that would resist her. She had given her heart to idolatry that led to selfishness and self-deceit. Baal and Asherah worship demanded loyalty even to the sacrifice of the worshiper's own children. You can imagine what turmoil of emotions could run unchecked in a mother's heart at having to choose such barbarous practices. Instead of choosing Jehovah, who promised blessing, peace, and unconditional love, she chose to follow a self-seeking god of revenge, hatred, and destruction.

An unchecked heart produces childlike tantrums and methods to try and control those around you. Jezebel needed to listen to the rhythm of her soul. If she had, she would have realized she was out of control. She was so incredibly blind to it that even moments before her death she thought she could control her own servants, with their loyalty protecting her from death. She fixed her face and hair and stood in a window, preening as King Jehu, whom God had anointed as king over Israel to destroy the house of Ahab, arrived. I think the servants had enough of her spoiled-brat attitude and obeyed King Jehu, who ordered them to throw her down. They pushed her from her window and she was trampled under the hooves of Jehu's war horse. (2 Kings 9:30–37). Even in her death she was desecrated; as Elijah had prophesied, her flesh was eaten by dogs. What a humiliating demise. Talk about not finishing well! It makes me shudder and motivates me to pay attention to my heart.

Proverbs says that we are to, "Above all else, guard your heart, for everything you do flows from it" (Proverbs 4:23). Another translation says, "It determines the course of your life." A few verses prior to that important verse says, "But the way of the wicked is like the deep darkness; they don't know what makes them stumble" (4:19 NLT). I would say that this verse in Proverbs sums up Jezebel's life. Her heart was so deceived by her idol worship she couldn't identify what made her so wicked. She had so many tangled issues in her life they created a web of self-deceit that hardened her heart. Her leadership was void of anything pure and holy because of her unresolved issues.

Listen to the context of this very significant truth of guarding our hearts in Proverbs 4:20–27 (HCSB).

My son, pay attention to my words;
listen closely to my sayings.

Don't lose sight of them;
keep them within your heart.

For they are life to those who find them,
and health to one's whole body.

Guard your heart above all else,
for it is the source of life.

Don't let your mouth speak dishonestly,
and don't let your lips talk deviously.

Let your eyes look forward;
fix your gaze straight ahead.

Carefully consider the path for your feet,
and all your ways will be established.

Don't turn to the right or to the left;
keep your feet away from evil.

God can redeem our past for our future. He gives us the tools and resources to be able to walk on a straight path. These gems of truth are proof that God has practical ways and means to instruct us to move in the right direction. Here is a list from this passage we all can follow to make sure we are guarding our heart from either falling prey to our past or giving up and settling for a life of mediocrity.

1. DON'T LOSE SIGHT—Write them on your heart. In other words, we need to keep reminding ourselves of the truth. Our human nature is to gravitate to the negative. Keep God's truth's close by where you can access it. I like to have a small Bible close by me at all times. I have in seasons also carried with me a small notebook and 3-by-5 cards with Scripture on them to help me remember the truth God desires to brand into my heart.

2. GUARD MY HEART—Jezebel had incredible idol worship in her life. It distracted her heart from all that is pure and good.

What idols in your life distract you from guarding your heart? My iPhone, iPad, and computer can be idols in my life, by depending on them too much. Really! It can be a huge issue for me. Entertainment, friendships, shopping (ouch), and many other things can keep us from guarding our hearts if we are not careful.

3. SPEAK HONESTLY AND TRUTHFULLY—I fear today just listening in on conversations of believers and the secular world that sometimes there seems to be very little difference between us. I am not referring to whether there are words peppered in the conversation such as *blessed, sanctification,* or even *church.* It is in the everyday conversations of what makes our lives stand apart. Christians unfortunately today don't have a very good reputation when it comes to our speech of integrity. We should be leading the way with integrity of our word, being on time, following through with commitments, and others. I have been really challenged in this area the last few years recognizing that people are watching me because of whom I claim I belong to, Jesus Christ. I need to make sure I mean what I say and say what I mean with integrity.

4. KEEP LOOKING FORWARD, EYES FIXED STRAIGHT AHEAD— This is a huge reminder to me not to dwell in the past, but look to the future. Deal with the past as God presents the opportunity but then press forward, anticipating the future. Too often we stay stuck in the past because it is where we are most comfortable. You can't see behind you if you actually

fix your eyes straight ahead, unless you have eyes in the back of your head. If you have trouble with this, ask God to give you something to help fix your eyes ahead. Hold on to the truth like Paul says in Philippians 3:12–14 (HCSB). He knows he hasn't arrived yet, but can take hold of the future, because "I also have been taken hold of by Christ Jesus." I love that. We can do it because Jesus has His hold on us! He then gives the steps to take in order to be able to embrace that truth. "But one thing I do; forgetting what is behind and reaching forward to what is ahead." We may never forget our past, but that word in Philippians, "forgetting," implies that we are no longer to care for the past, we are to neglect it and change our thinking to look forward.

5. STAY ON THE PATH—Don't turn to the right or the left; keep your feet away from evil. Have you ever ended up somewhere you didn't really intend to go? In order to stay on the path and not turn to the right or the left, we need to follow the four steps above. Our feet will only go where our mind gives the signal to go here or to go there. If we stay on the path, our feet will stand firm in where God wants us to be to move forward, and in the process be able to guard our heart!

We must diligently guard our hearts so that we can nurture the godly truths God wants to instill deep within us. We don't have to resolve ourselves to the pain of our past in order to make an impact. Can I say this to you? Believe God, and in believing God, He will make a way for your past to be redeemed for your future!

I want to close this chapter with the story of my friend, whom I have witnessed being lifted out of the ugly pit of her past to a life-giving ministry and future. When I first met Esther she wore a veneer of having the need to prove herself in ministry. She appeared on the outside to be happy and fulfilled, but she was really feeling extremely insecure and inadequate. She often presented herself as confident, but underneath there was an uncertainty and extreme feelings of unworthiness even though she was a fully surrendered, mature believer.

Esther and I took a course together that was designed to help chart the future and create clarity. It was a three-day intensive in which you peeled off the layers of your life to evaluate, examine, and discover how to write a mission and vision statement according to your gifts, values, and life experiences. We each had been given a half sheet of poster board to make a chronological timeline of events in our lives. The first day we listed primary events and relationships on yellow sticky notes and attached them to the board. The second day we were instructed to look over all that we had written and exchange some of those yellow events for a new color, pink. The pink sticky notes would represent the pain in our lives.

Esther got stuck; she became overwhelmed at the pink that covered her board. She cried, and cried, actually sobbed uncontrollably at one point and had to leave the room. As she tried to get her emotions under control, the facilitator had to stop our session because we knew God was doing something extraordinary and wanted to wait for her so she wouldn't miss anything.

Esther had enormous pain in her life from years of hiding a secret that was destroying her ability to be an emotionally whole and healthy person. She lived with the secret of having been sexually abused as a child. She was abused in the church by some of the leadership and had carried the burden of not being able to reveal her secret for fear of rejection and abandonment. The process was for Esther a necessary journey for her past and the shaping of her future. That day was another piece of the long, hard road to healing and recovery.

Esther emerged a new person full of hope and discovered a depth of joy that she hadn't experienced before. Looking back she shared that she had succeeded as a leader in ministry but was failing at home. It was time to address the issue fully and head on. From that intensive three-day seminar she made a decision to step away for a short season to dig deep and give herself permission to grieve her past as a part of the healing process. It was the door to her past being unlocked that led to a ministry that has blessed hundreds, if not thousands, of men and women.

Esther served for several years as director of a recovery ministry, a Christ-centered 12-step program that enables people who are caught in the pain of their past from abuse, addictions, and other behaviors that keep people in bondage. Esther is a vibrant leader and is genuine in her love to support people who have been enslaved to their addictions and their past. In her words, she has "come to know God to be the restorer, to bring people out the shame of darkness into the light." She is a woman who has overcome the myth, GOD CAN'T USE ME BECAUSE OF

MY PAST. God has not only used her in amazing ways, but her life has had a ripple effect that is beyond our ability to measure. No longer shackled by the chains of her past, she is thriving.

Lord, where are my unresolved issues? I want to lead fully in emotional strength and health. Give me Your perspective. Thank You that you have woven my life in a tapestry of threads that includes my mistakes and failures. Lead me, Jesus. Right now I submit to You to hear what I may not want to hear but need to.

THIS IS OUT OF MY COMFORT ZONE

Myth 4

Leading Outside the Box

JAEL

"When you come to the end of your rope, tie a knot and hang on."
—FRANKLIN ROOSEVELT

I was tingling with an adrenaline rush as I sent a text to my youngest son, Jason. "I did it, Jason," I simply stated. I had just taken a step that was for me an outside-the-box, grand physical feat. Moments before, I had just been released out of a secure harness after experiencing the longest zip line in North America in RockRidge Canyon, British Columbia. I had allowed myself to be strapped into a hefty harness and zipped down hundreds of feet over a lake and tall trees on a steel wire that probably was no more than an inch in diameter. I have to confess I screamed the whole three minutes I was zipping through the sky. I am not sure if I screamed because of sheer terror or the exhilaration of conquering a very great fear of heights.

This was the third time I had been at RockRidge Canyon, each time having the privilege of being the guest speaker for a women's retreat. This time, however, I was the guest speaker for my own church women's retreat and I knew I would never hear the end of it if I didn't take up the adventure. After all, these were the women who knew me best, and had great expectations from their pastor's wife. Normally I am not one to cave to peer pressure. It happened subtly as I was standing in line to get my lunch after our morning session. Carolyn, one of our young adult staff members, sheepishly asked me if I was going on the zip line. I told her my tale, and she said she wanted to conquer her fear as well. I am not sure what happened but the words jumped out of my mouth, "Let's do it together!"

Next thing I knew, I was standing at the sign-up table and receiving my wristband for admission. After lunch, Carolyn and I hiked up to the platform. We didn't have time to think about being afraid because the steep hike was one that caused you to feel like you needed oxygen at the top. I looked at our "experts" who were going to strap us in and give us instructions. They weren't any older than my youngest son, who was 21 at the time. I nervously asked them if they really knew what they were doing and how much they loved their mothers and to pretend that I was their mom who wanted to be alive at the end of the ride. They responded with looks of, is she for real? (Did I tell you I get real chatty when I am nervous?)

We had two options: to either sit and go down the zip line or be hooked up at the back of the harness to fly like Superman. I knew this was probably the only time I could get the nerve up to do something like this, so I went all out. I wanted to fly! They fit us into our harness and gave us instructions, short for "we accept no liability if you don't have a good experience." I can't tell you what a surreal feeling it is to be standing on a platform hundreds of feet up in the air with a little gate in front of you, knowing that when that gate opens, you will have lost total control, your feet leaving solid ground. In the last of the instructions, Carolyn froze up and wasn't sure she wanted to zip. That only gave me more courage; after all, I was supposed to be the older, more mature one. I tried to convince both of us as I was talking at warp speed (remember the nervous part) that it would be over in three minutes.

We counted to three, ran off the platform, the gate was open, and we flew, over the tops of trees, over the lake, over the screaming fans below. Before we landed I was crying, because I had stepped out of my comfort zone and experienced the thrill of adventure into the unknown. I kept saying, "Thank You, God, thank You, and thank You," as they lowered me to safety.

When my son received the text message, he was stunned in disbelief that his own mother had done something so brave. (Are you getting the picture that I am not the woodsy, outdoorsy, adventure-seeking type?) He congratulated me. Being the mother of all sons, it made me feel like I had just crossed the wild wilderness like the pioneer women 150 years ago. I had stepped out of the box and out of my comfort zone!

TIME TO BE A GROWN-UP

As I write, the ground is covered with snow and shoppers are hastily making last-minute purchases before Christmas. As I look out my window, the street looks picture-perfect, with twinkling lights and the snow glistening in the moonlight. It looks like any other year, but this year is significantly different than last year. We are in a serious global financial crisis. The day-to-day news is grim with job losses, home foreclosures, retailers' woes, and the volatility of the stock market. The news isn't much brighter in the church community. Churches are compromising their biblical stand, doors are closing, and leaders are stepping down. The seemingly familiar, convenient standing on middle ground for Christians is being put to the test. "It's time to be a grown-up," one financial commentator said in an article on how to weather these tough times.

Being a grown-up is leaving our warm, comfortable place of familiarity and being willing to venture out into the unknown. Shattering the myth of This Is Out of My Comfort Zone challenges us to think outside the box in where God is leading us on our journey. It's time to wake up instead of nuzzling deeper into what's comfortable or what feels good to us. As we have already discussed in previous chapters, God is rallying women who will listen and be willing to trust Him in stepping into the unknown. He is looking for women who will believe Him, trust Him, and follow Him to undiscovered territory of ministry and action to a world that is searching for, more importantly needing, hope in the midst of uncertainty and turmoil.

An Outside-the-Box Kind of Woman

Deborah, a judge in Israel, wrote a song in the Book of Judges paying tribute to a woman who nearly single-handedly took down a formidable enemy for the nation of Israel. Her life was obscure, but her story is compelling in understanding how God often calls His people to do "out of the box" opportunities to change the world. Deborah is singing her tribute in Judges 5:24–27. The lyrics of her song tell the story of Jael.

> *Most blessed of women be Jael,*
> *the wife of Heber the Kenite,*
> *most blessed of tent-dwelling women.*
>
> *He asked for water, and she gave him milk;*
> *in a bowl fit for nobles she brought him curdled milk.*
>
> *Her hand reached for the tent peg,*
> *her right hand for the workman's hammer.*
> *She struck Sisera, she crushed his head,*
> *she shattered and pierced his temple.*
>
> *At her feet he sank,*
> *he fell; there he lay.*
> *At her feet he sank, he fell;*
> *where he sank, there he fell—dead.*

Deborah was the appointed leader of Israel at that time. She had been given a God-sized assignment of bringing the armies of Israel against their oppressors the Canaanites. God had given the Israelites over to them because of their hardened hearts and evil actions. They were battered and bruised cruelly by King

Jabin and they cried out to God. God in His compassion heard their cries and Deborah boldly led the army with Barak to defeat the Canaanites. When the enemy was dispersed, they scattered. Sisera, the commander in chief, abandoned his chariot and fled on foot. He approached what he thought was a friendly hiding place only to meet his death at the hands of a woman named Jael.

Talk about stepping outside the box and your comfort zone! This was no easy task for a woman. To take a tent peg and a hammer with steely resolve and approach a sleeping commander to perform such a grisly act is not exactly a feminine task. It is uncharacteristic. She had more than courage, she had guts. As Sisera approached the tent, she told him, "Come my lord, come right in. Don't be afraid" (Judges 4:18). He had just seen his whole army slaughtered with not one man left alive. He was truly running for his life and thought he would be safe. But God had other plans. He used a woman who was willing to act outside of her comfort zone and do an outside-the-box feat to accomplish His purposes. I don't think nailing tent pegs into human skulls was an everyday chore for Jael. I am sure she had not done that before. She might have used her tools and pounding the pegs into the ground to set up the tent. She evidently knew who the enemy was and God led her to defeat him for all of Israel.

One of the most astonishing things I notice in this story is the fact that God used the tools and resources that were available to Jael to carry out His plan. He didn't ask her to use something that she wasn't skilled at or completely unfamiliar with. She had most likely used that hammer several times and probably had pounded tent pegs in more times than she could count.

She knew how to use them with precision and accuracy. How else could she have been brave enough to do the horrific deed? I bet she hadn't ever thought that she would wake up that day and take down the commander of the army with her common, ordinary tools.

Here is the point. When God nudges you to step out of our comfort zone and do something outside the box, He will most likely use the tools that are already in your hand. It will just be different than you have used them before.

In nearly 30 years of being in ministry, I have been involved in several different leadership roles, and many times have felt way out of my comfort zone. There is one common thread I can count on. God has most often used what is already in my hand, meaning my life experiences, my gifts, and talents. It doesn't mean, however, that I am fully confident in accessing those resources; it just means they are resources God has provided for me to equip me for the assignment. It is what is in my hand at the moment.

My hammer and tent pegs that I have been working with already are my qualifications to do the job to which He has called me. That is how I know I can trust Him as I step outside the lines of what I think I am most comfortable in doing. I just have to look at what's in my hand and call on God to empower me to do the rest. I often don't even know the outcome, or even the final steps, before the assignment is over, but God always seems to give me exactly what I need with what He has already provided for me. To be honest, I find it both exhilarating and frightening as I approach a God-sized mission. Now to be extremely truthful, many times it has me feeling anxious.

I am learning to just do it afraid, and trust God for that first plunge into uncharted territory. It is kind of like that first step off the platform of the zip line. My stomach bottomed out and my heart was in my throat; but after that, it was a thrilling ride that matched no other I had experienced.

From Platform to Safe Haven

On a cool autumn day in 2004, my friend Scharme read an article about children and sex slavery. Until then she had been totally unaware that any kind of slavery existed. As she read the personal stories, she felt as if her heart were being ripped out. In a phrase, she was wrecked. At that moment she promised the Lord she would do anything to help bring an end to modern-day sex slavery. That year her Christmas gift to the Lord was to help rescue at least one woman and one girl.

And so began the journey as one of six ordinary women living in comfortable suburbia deciding to take a trip to Southeast Asia visiting several World Concern projects. What they saw changed their lives dramatically. The reality of extreme poverty and the exploitation of young girls and boys being driven into the modern-day sex trade by their hopeless circumstances forever made a mark on these women. Their hearts shattered as they learned that often these children are being sold by their own families, a measure of the desperation their parents felt. The horror of this modern-day slavery goes beyond such life-threatening diseases as HIV/AIDS and hepatitis; it means irreparable damage to their tender souls and loss of their innocent childhoods.

On their journey the women met the director of the Cambodia Hope Organization. They discovered that the director knows firsthand about child slavery. He was in a child labor camp for three years under the Khmer Rouge regime. After seeing what he was already doing after only a couple of years in his role, they asked if there was anything else he might need that they could provide. Just before they left he drew on a napkin a picture of his dream, Safe Haven, a transitional home for those rescued from slave trafficking.

After praying and talking together, when they returned home they decided that was something they could do. This group of women came home determined to never forget what they had seen and decided to join with World Concern and their partner Cambodia Hope Organization to provide programs that teach men and women life skills so they aren't forced to choose a life of begging or slavery into prostitution. They began a group, Women of Purpose, now known as the ministry Frontline for Justice. They meet regularly to implement plans for fund-raising projects, and for prevention and protection strategies for women and children at risk.

Scharme discovered a purpose beyond her comfort zone. She is driven by what she and others experienced firsthand and compelled to help stop the horror of exploitation of women and children. When she was interviewed by a local television news station, she was asked why she was choosing to help people from across the globe. She replied tearfully that she had prayed, "Lord, I will do anything You ask me to do. I have grandchildren the same ages as these children that are being trafficked into slavery."

I have known Scharme for several years. She has been a faithful wife, mother, grandmother, and humble servant in the church where her husband was pastor. Scharme would never refer to herself as a leader and has faithfully served behind the scenes in many different capacities. But God is raising her up to lead other women to be a voice for those who have no voice. Since that first trip in 2005, they have made several subsequent trips and raised hundreds of thousands of dollars toward the vision, Safe Haven, a dream that they first witnessed scribbled on a napkin. Frontline for Justice has worked tirelessly to assist him to purchase land and build the project Safe Haven. It is now completed, giving the opportunity for children to be in a safe environment and provide education for life skills to help end the cycle of poverty and slavery that these children have known. The larger vision is to multiply churches all along the Cambodia/Thailand border. This will provide a basis for replicating other Safe Havens and training centers.

One of Scharme's strengths is the ability to nurture. She is one of the most amazing mothers I have ever known. Having struggled with feelings of inadequacy in other areas she has flourished with strength in nurturing others. She is a leader who is using the tools and resources that have been in her hand, her gifts to nurture and influence. Scharme would say she is no great orator, but when you listen to her talk about her passion, you feel compelled to do something! She is using what is in her hand to inspire ordinary women like herself to think outside the box and step out in faith to rescue children, providing them with hope that they might not have otherwise. Scharme sees herself as a modern-day abolitionist and has boldly stated that she will do everything within her means to fight this battle and see sex slavery come to an end. Is it out of her comfort zone? Yes! Is it leading outside the box? Yes, but with her hammer and her tent peg, Scharme is changing the world one life at a time.

How do you respond when God asks you do accomplish something that is uncharacteristic?

Lord, I confess I like to be comfortable. I don't like to be pushed out of my comfort zone. Give me the courage to do it afraid if need be. Show me, like Jael, what is in my hand and lead me to complete the assignment You have for me.

Chapter 9

Leading in Transition

RUTH

*"Twenty years from now you will be more disappointed by
the things that you didn't do than by the ones you did do. So
throw off the bowlines. Sail away from the safe harbor. Catch
the trade winds in your sails. Explore. Dream. Discover."*
—Mark Twain

H i, Mrs. Beyer," several children chorused, crowding around
her during recess as she was making her way to her office.
Mrs. Beyer is somewhat of a star personality in the realm of
education where she lives. Mrs. Beyer, as she is known to students and staff, is Debbie Beyer, founder and executive director of Literacy First Charter Schools, in East County San Diego,
California. Debbie had a dream as a young adult to create her
own school. Today that dream is a reality. Currently there are
four schools in four different locations, kindergarten through
high school, under Debbie's direction. Literacy Charter Schools
are exceptional and have been nominated as a California Distin-
guished School. Debbie is overwhelmingly persistent in working

toward her goal and leads with expectations of implementing excellence for herself, her teachers, students, and staff. Debbie has learned through personal adversity and career detours that any dream worth hanging onto comes at a great cost.

More than 16 years ago she found herself in the middle of a nightmare. Through no fault of her own, the stability she knew as a wife, mother, and educator was suddenly ripped out from under her. The nightmare escalated and she was left alone as a single mother to raise and provide for her three young boys. Her dream stayed tucked away deep in her heart as she tried to make sense of the sudden transition in her once seemingly perfect world.

It took her years to overcome the obstacles, but Debbie is a person of action, not a quitter. She knows who fights for her, and believes in a God who has a book full of promises to impart to those who would just believe Him at His Word. Debbie is a visionary leader and those who work with her not only sit up and listen, they are keen to follow her leadership. Her drive to live with purpose is contagious and she lives this mantra "because it matters" when asked why she does what she does. She is a cheerleader to her family, friends, and staff. Debbie is cut from the kind of cloth where greatness inspires others to action.

On one of my visits, she relayed a story to me about the expansion of the new schools. "I have never been so out on a limb in my life. I feel so inadequate," she told me. She then spoke of "having it out with God" on her way to an event, telling Him she didn't feel equipped or adequate to do the job, not to mention other feelings of helplessness. It was during this time of discouragement that God sent a woman Debbie had never met before to deliver a message. The woman approached her inquiring if she was Mrs. Beyer, the "star." She went on to say that she was a Christian and said that God had directed her to pray over her. She addressed Debbie as "Deborah, woman of wisdom" in her prayer and spoke to every obstacle with which she had confronted God earlier that morning, and empowered her through prayer toward the next step. She was overcome with God's personal response to her earlier doubts. She knew at that moment that whatever it would take, God had assured her this was His dream for her life and He would give her exactly what she needed to accomplish the assignment. Debbie Beyer is a woman with a mission; she is changing one community at a time through the vehicle of education, shaping young minds and developing future leaders for tomorrow.

BECOMING A PERSON OF ACTION

When we are in transition, it is easy to fall into limbo and experience decision paralysis. When life takes a detour, it's easy to lose hope and our ability to make a wise decision. Our expectation scale can move drastically in the direction of "what's the use, if this is all there is." At that moment we have a choice. We can choose to move ahead with uncharacteristic persistence or we can let the obstacles overcome us and settle into "this is way out of my comfort zone," and give up. I believe this is the critical place in our journey of coming face-to-face with our destiny and which path we will choose; one of our own making to try and salvage the detour to get to our destination, or trusting God that He knows what He is doing in orchestrating the big picture of our lives. Transition is disconcerting, it is hard, and it can feel like our dreams are being taken away. But transition is also the place that reveals what we are made of. It unmasks the exterior of our heart attitudes. What oozes out during a season of transition can be all too revealing. The next step, once we are confronted with the transition, is monumental in our decision process. We can't freeze up. We have to take action.

Andy Andrews in his book *The Traveler's Gift* describes the character of someone who chooses to be a person of action.

"I am a person of action. I can make a decision. I can make it now. A person who moves neither left nor right is destined for mediocrity. When faced with a decision, many people say they are waiting for God. But I understand, in most cases God is waiting for me! I am a person of action." What I hear Andy saying is that we can't allow obstacles of any kind to paralyze us from taking action toward the next steps.

GPS

A map is a necessity when you are in a strange city, don't you think? Being in transition is like visiting a new city; it is unfamiliar. Navigating through uncharted territory can be daunting at best. Having a GPS in your car or on your cell phone can make a trip less stressful or even save your marriage! Too often Kevin and I have arrived at our destination tired, hungry, and just wanting to go to sleep. We are both leaders and used to giving direction. Finding our hotel or a restaurant can test us relationally to the limit as we attempt to work together. Kevin and I have vowed that what we really need to de-stress when we arrive in a new city is to invest in a GPS. We arrived at that decision after flying almost 22 hours to reach Sydney, Australia. We were visiting our son, who was attending Hillsong College. We picked up our car and tried to orient ourselves for driving on the opposite side of the road. We had what we thought were clear directions, only to find out later they were faulty. We drove around and around, literally in the same two-mile circle, for more than an hour in an attempt to find our hotel. It was maddening to say the least. Finally exasperated, I suggested we ask someone. That proved futile, either because we weren't able to acclimate to the Aussie accent or were so tired we became confused. Exhausted, we stumbled into the Hillsong Church parking lot and happened upon our son Jason as he was leaving church. Like an experienced tour guide, he led us to our hotel, where we crashed after being up for more than 24 hours.

When we are in transition, having some clear direction can be extremely advantageous. I like to adopt my own kind of GPS—God Proves Sovereign. No matter how many times life takes a turn and creates a bend in the road that I don't expect, God in His sovereignty reassures me that He isn't surprised and is aware of what's happening in my life. Relying on my GPS in my car gives me a sense a security, knowing I will actually get to my destination. The God kind of GPS affords me something far greater—the opportunity to relax and trust even if I don't know where the next turn will be.

Ruth the Moabitess found herself in a glaring life transition and in need of a GPS. She was a young widow who had journeyed to a foreign country with her widowed mother-in-law, Naomi. Ruth had committed to staying with her and caring for her all the days of her life. She left everything that was "safe" to her behind in Moab by adopting Naomi's heritage. Ruth vowed, "Your people will be my people and your God my God. Where you die I will die, and there I will be buried. May the Lord deal with me, be it ever so severely, if anything but death separates you and me" (Ruth 1:16-17).

Seeping out of the cracks of transition in Ruth's life came grace and honor toward her mother-in-law. It wasn't important for her to know the next step at that juncture. It was important for her to understand her identity in the transition, whom she belonged to—Naomi and the Lord God. Even though Naomi pleaded with both Ruth and her sister-in-law, Orpah, to stay in Moab, Ruth was determined to follow Naomi. If we peek around the corner in the story of these Scriptures, it appears that Ruth was drawn to Jehovah God through Naomi's influence because of what she committed to, even accepting the consequences if she broke her vow (vv. 16 and 17). It could be because she lived with Naomi and her family for ten years and observed the worship of the one true God. Elimelech, Naomi's husband, being the family patriarch, most likely influenced her along with Naomi to forsake her own gods from Moab.

When you and I are in transition, it is easy to forget who we are. When our world gets turned upside down we can get confused and lose sight of why we are doing what we are doing.

A life-altering episode happened in my journey of leadership in 2004. I was at the most exhilarating and rewarding time I could be as a leader. Our call to Canada seemed to be revealing God's purposes over my life. God had birthed a dream in the core of my soul to lead a team of women that would have a national impact toward empowering and encouraging women in leadership.

I began to see God unfolding the dream in the years prior. I had in my heart to draw women together from all denominations to train, equip, and encourage them to go back into their communities to leave a lasting imprint. We as a team had witnessed our city and region come together in unity, culminating in a three-day conference for women. We had 149 churches represented and 10 organizations. Beth Moore and other special guest speakers, including nearly 30 leaders from North America, came to breathe hope and encourage the women in our city. God birthed it in a supernatural way, and we saw God's Spirit fall in a way that was far beyond what we had ever witnessed at a women's event. In the midst of that, I had been invited to work at Focus on the Family Canada to do a research project to launch a national ministry to encourage women leaders across Canada in hopes of strengthening what was happening in the local churches. After the conference, I began traveling across North America interviewing women in leadership from denominations and organizations to get the heartbeat of women leaders and find the missing link for women leaders needing resources and encouragement.

Focus on the Family Canada was a wonderful organization to work for when we lived in Canada. I was thriving and it was a good fit. Those in my department were excited about how God was going to lead us to make a difference for women. I would wake up nearly every day pinching myself. *It doesn't get any better than this. I am living my dream.* And it certainly was an Ephesians 3:20 season, "above all I could ask or imagine." I felt so humbled that God had given me the privilege to speak into the lives of women across Canada. Wow! I was humbled beyond anything. At the end of the project the Lord revealed a specific strategy as I waited upon Him through prayer and soaking up His Word. As the deadline approached for the report to be completed and to be presented to the executive leadership team, we were anticipating the soon-to-be launching of a new initiative for women leaders.

And then it happened. I was called into the vice-president's office and I was told that for a number of reasons they had to cut some programming and would not be launching our new initiative for women in leadership. There were hot-burner issues regarding the family in Canada that needed to be priority. Sitting in the office, it seemed surreal. Was I hearing it right? This couldn't be. I was in shock to say the least. I have great respect for Focus on the Family and understood the decision they had to make. It was a tough call for them to make, but I was devastated.

I found myself faced with a crisis of belief. Did I hear God right? Had I made a mistake coming to Focus on the Family? While losing my job at Focus, we faced some external crisis and pressures. Our family was in three car accidents in the course of a month. So as I was nursing my physical body, my heart was grieving as well. God ministered to me from His Word and gave me a challenge from Numbers 20, the story when Moses didn't trust God enough to demonstrate His holiness; God said he would not enter the land. I sensed God was saying, "Pay attention to this; this has important implications for your life—for you to reach your promised land."

So in the midst of the pain both physical and emotional, as I cried out to Him, God gave me gushing streams in the desert from His Word. I began to review and reflect on the spiritual markers in my life of God's calling. And the Lord began to affirm that through Scripture, prayer, and affirmation from other people. Then on March 6, 2005, I had an encounter with God in Psalm 37:3–7.

> Trust in the LORD and do good;
> dwell in the land and enjoy safe pasture.
>
> Delight yourself in the LORD
> and he will give you the desires of your heart.
>
> Commit your way to the LORD;
> trust in him and he will do this:

He will make your righteousness shine like the dawn,
the justice of your cause like the noonday sun.

Be still before the LORD and wait patiently for him.

As I sat in my chair and wept, God's Spirit began to speak to me about trusting Him. And He began to impart to me that He was going to lead me on a deeper journey of trust than I had known before. As I was crying, I felt God asking me, "What do you need right now?" As I told Him, I had a sense of God's presence like a blanket enfolding me into His great love. And I leaned into His embrace to trust Him in a new way.

I learned four things as I meditated on this psalm for several weeks. Maybe you will find yourself in between the lines of what I learned.

1. TRUST IN THE LORD AND DO WELL.

What does it mean to trust? It means to believe Him, take Him at His Word, and hope in His promises. I adopted this pledge to remind myself during that time of what God expects of me in transition.

MY FIVE-STATEMENT PLEDGE OF TRUST

(1) I will choose to TRUST God even if I don't understand.

(2) I will believe God, for He is TRUSTWORTHY.

(3) I will WAIT expectantly as I TRUST.

(4) I will confess that my HOPE and TRUST are in the living God.

(5) I will walk in humility as I TRUST God for the future.

2. Dwell in the land and enjoy safe pasture.

Dwelling in the land means to be content with the assignment that God has given you and me right now in the moment. Live in the moment, in God's presence, even if you don't have clarity for the next step. Staying in your assignment is your protection over your life. What happens when you go outside your assignment and take on a mission that God hasn't intended? It produces anxiety, undue weariness, and a type of striving or performing to gain identity that may become lost in the confusion. Remember Ruth? Cling to her example. She was willing to abandon everything to be secure in the identity of what she knew to be true—the relationship she had with Naomi and Naomi's God. Trust in God's faithful track record. He will move you to the next pasture when the timing is right, when the grass is flourishing for you to benefit the most from God's purposes and His assignment for you.

3. Delight in the Lord.

What does it mean to delight in the Lord? I really wrestled with this one. I didn't want to overspiritualize and yet there are simple, pure truths found in the list I discovered as I looked up similar passages. I challenge you to pull out your concordance and do the same. I will list a few to get you started. The list might surprise you in what you find we are to delight in!

Delight in His law (seven times in my concordance).
Delight in deliverance.
Delight in revering His name.

Delight in the Almighty.
Delight in salvation.
Delight in vindication.
Delight in God's works.
Delight in the path or your commands.
Delight in rejoicing in His presence.
Delight in weakness, in insults, in hardships, in persecutions,
  in difficulties.

4. Wait patiently, expectantly.

Part of the condition of waiting is first is to be *still*. I don't have to remind you how difficult it is to wait. Waiting is hard for our culture; we don't want to wait for anything. Waiting in line is a cramp in our time schedule. We are instructed to *wait* on the Lord. What exactly does that mean when you are in transition? For me it meant not to peddle my vision or manipulate to try and make things happen. Oh, I hate to even admit to you how many times I have done that! It's embarrassing. God was very clear to me on that point. I was to be still and wait on Him. It wasn't an enormous wait; it was a mere few months. In the interim, I read books, prayed, and invited others into my journey. I have to tell you, though, there have been other times in my life that I have waited much longer than a few months. I am learning that the longer God wants me to wait, the deeper the treasure I discover in that time.

God began to speak and move as I waited. He called me to take action one baby step at a time. Remember the earlier quote from Andy Andrews about taking action? He said,

"Sometimes God is waiting for us." I do advocate stepping out in faith, even boldly, but in confidence that it is God who is nudging me and not my own selfish motives to regain my identity. One of the critical things God reminded me of was this, who I was and what was my identity wrapped up in? Was it wrapped up in what I was doing, or was my identity rooted in God? Was it about God or about me? These were important questions I could answer only in the stillness of my soul laid bare before my creator.

Psalm 37:5 clearly says, "Commit your way to the Lord, trust in Him and He will do this." That word *trust* in that verse is like a bookend in the psalmist's instruction. In his book *Ruthless Trust*, Brennan Manning says,

> The way of trust is a movement into obscurity into the undefined, into ambiguity, not into some pre-determined, clearly delineated plan for the future. The next step discloses itself only out of a discernment of God acting in the desert of the present moment. The reality of naked trust is the life of a pilgrim who leaves what is nailed down, obvious and secure, and walks into the unknown without any rational explanation to justify the decision or guarantee the future. Why? Because God has signaled the movement and offered His presence and promise.

What do you need to trust God for today? Your ministry? Something big and ominous that you have no control over? Something in your personal life? A relationship? Ruth set the example for us; she walked into the unknown out of her comfort zone but with decisive action to trust the God of her beloved mother-in-law.

Lord, help me to remember in transition that my identity is rooted in You and not what I do. Once again help me to trust in Your GPS and to hold on to the promises that You are sovereign no matter what bend in the road I encounter. Help me to be comfortable in the moment of the unknown because You are the guide.

I DON'T HAVE ENOUGH EXPERIENCE

Myth 5

Chapter 10

Leading Out of Holiness

EZEKIEL

*"Too much caution is bad for you. It is usually wiser to stand up
to a scary-seeming experience and walk right into it,
risking the bruises or hard knocks. You are likely to find it is not
as tough as you had thought. Or you may find it plenty tough,
but also discover you have what it takes to handle it."*

—NORMAN VINCENT PEALE

The obstacle I face the most when trying to empower leaders
is trying to debunk this last myth, I DON'T HAVE ENOUGH
EXPERIENCE. To begin to unpack this let me ask you a question.
What do you think it takes to stay on the cutting edge of
leadership? I would like to plant some seeds for you to think
about when you find yourself stumbling over this obstacle when
trying to move forward.

Here it is. Are you ready? More than reading the latest books
on leadership, gaining more knowledge, and seeking out greater
tools to use with those you lead, the way to stay on the cutting
edge and be relevant is to begin each day like this: Set this book

down, get on your knees, and confess to God your desperation to have Him be *your personal leader* in this process. Tell Him how much you love Him and believe that as He has called you to lead He will direct you as you seek Him. It is all about surrender.

Oswald Chambers says this about surrender, "If we are truly surrendered, we will never be aware of our own efforts to remain surrendered. Our entire life will be consumed with the One to whom we surrender." This should be our heart's cry every moment of the day.

Do you want to know how you can measure your effectiveness and be assured that you are making a difference? Make these verses in Deuteronomy your prayer for your endeavors whether in the church, community, workplace, or a nonprofit ministry:

> *So Moses told the people, "You must obey all the commands of the LORD your God, following his instructions in every detail. Stay on the path that the LORD your God has commanded you to follow. Then you will live long and prosperous lives in the land you are about to enter and occupy"*
> (Deuteronomy 5:32–33 NLT).

My dear sister, that is the ultimate core of being a success as God views success, following His instructions in every detail and staying on the path that God has commanded you and me to follow! At the risk of the above suggestion sounding too simplistic, I also encourage leaders to read, attend conferences, and interact with other leaders, but only *after* we have made an intentional effort to surrender. It is important to develop your gifts, but not at the expense of surrendering those gifts to the One who gave them to you and me in the first place.

We have it backwards at times. We rely on all the great leadership tools as we strive to be what we think we need to be because of our insecurities. We can have an "I DON'T HAVE ENOUGH EXPERIENCE" attitude that fuels the striving. If God calls you, then He obviously thinks you have the experience you need at the moment to accomplish His purposes for the mission. He will supply the rest! Stay on the path.

TRUE SPIRITUAL LEADERSHIP

A few years ago I had the privilege of being part of a seminar titled "Spiritual Leadership" with Henry Blackaby, who wrote the best-selling Bible study *Experiencing God*. We were gathered as leaders to explore the topic, "What Does a Spiritual Leader Look Like?" Blackaby said, "Spiritual leaders move people onto God's agenda." Read that phrase again and let it sink in. I know I wrote it down at the time and have never forgotten the force of those words.

I might add that nothing is more important than spiritual leadership. It is even more important than experience or what we think experience should be! Can you hear what I am getting at? It's OK to feel like you don't have enough experience. God knows. He made you. He understands. He gets it that you need Him more than you need your experience. Blackaby went on to say that Christian leaders who know God and who know how to lead in a Christian manner will be phenomenally more effective in their world than even the most skilled and qualified leaders who lead without God.

There have been many times throughout the years that I have struggled with my own lack of qualifications. I never had the opportunity to graduate from college or seminary, but God has affirmed me over and over again as I have submitted to Him in obedience that He is the one who calls a leader and desires to do extraordinary things through a willing heart. It has only been the past 3 years that I have had the opportunity to go back to school. I recently graduated with my master's in leadership degree. Yahoo! Let me tell you, girlfriend, I felt old going back after nearly 30 years. But it was God's timing complementing this leadership season in my life and my window that God definitely planned.

As women called to lead, we are leading others prayerfully to discover their window of opportunity that God wants them to see. We help them to unlock their God-given dreams, gently pushing them to take a step. Living and operating under true spiritual leadership is essential for our maximum effectiveness.

One of the greatest temptations that we will face as leaders is to lead in our own strength. How do we stay guarded and alert to this temptation? We do so by making sure that we practice the principle of regularly examining our own hearts and lives. Holiness is more important than experience. When we focus on God, we will move people onto God's agenda and not our own.

A HARSH WARNING

I am going to deviate in the book from the female examples I have been using because I believe there is something exceptional that Ezekiel can say to us as leaders. God gave the spiritual leaders in Ezekiel's time an exhortation and warning. It would be helpful for us to engage the importance of this principle.

Let's paint the historical canvas first with a little background on the Book of Ezekiel in the Old Testament. Ezekiel's name means "God will strengthen." He was a sixth-century prophet during the time that the Israelites were taken captive by the Babylonians. God had called him to minister to Israel while they were in captivity. And He called Ezekiel specifically to be a "watchman on the wall," who in Scripture represents not a physical wall but a spiritual wall. God appointed him as a prophet to the exiles. If you know a little of Old Testament history, you will remember that God allowed them to be taken into captivity because they had walked away from God. He wanted Ezekiel to be their watchman and prophet to help them understand why they had been taken captive, and to bring a message of hope and a new awareness of their dependence on God.

Ezekiel lived in a time much like ours, a time of international crisis and conflict. His radical obedience to God caused him to illustrate God's messages dramatically. God needed someone who would "wake the dead," spiritually speaking, to remind them who God was. So God asked him to do things such as lie on his side for hundreds of days, to refrain from public weeping when his wife died as a symbolism of Israel's rebellion, and many other seemingly bizarre things.

We find more of what God was getting at specifically toward leaders in chapter 13 of Ezekiel. I want to warn you, these are harsh, sobering words that remind us that God takes those he appoints as leaders seriously.

Then this message came to me from the Lord: "Son of man, prophesy against the false prophets of Israel who are inventing their own prophecies. Say to them, 'Listen to the word of the Lord. This is what the Sovereign Lord says: What sorrow awaits the false prophets who are following their own imaginations and have seen nothing at all!'

"O people of Israel, these prophets of yours are like jackals digging in the ruins. They have done nothing to repair the breaks in the walls around the nation. They have not helped it to stand firm in battle on the day of the Lord. Instead, they have told lies and made false predictions. They say, 'This message is from the Lord,' even though the Lord never sent them. And yet they expect him to fulfill their prophecies! Can your visions be anything but false if you claim, 'This message is from the Lord,' when I have not even spoken to you?

"Therefore, this is what the Sovereign Lord says: Because what you say is false and your visions are a lie, I will stand against you, says the Sovereign Lord. I will raise my fist against all the prophets who see false visions and make lying predictions, and they

will be banished from the community of Israel. I will blot their names from Israel's record books, and they will never again set foot in their own land. Then you will know that I am the Sovereign Lord.

"This will happen because these evil prophets deceive my people by saying, 'All is peaceful' when there is no peace at all! It's as if the people have built a flimsy wall, and these prophets are trying to reinforce it by covering it with whitewash! Tell these whitewashers that their wall will soon fall down. A heavy rainstorm will undermine it; great hailstones and mighty winds will knock it down. And when the wall falls, the people will cry out, 'What happened to your whitewash?'

"Therefore, this is what the Sovereign Lord says: I will sweep away your whitewashed wall with a storm of indignation, with a great flood of anger, and with hailstones of fury. I will break down your wall right to its foundation, and when it falls, it will crush you. Then you will know that I am the Lord (Ezekiel 13:1–14 NLT).

I believe that if you are reading this book, you have good intentions as a child of God. You have the heart and passion to serve God with everything that you are. But sometimes we can get caught up in leading from our experiences and sabotage what God has destined for us. God is sovereign and can, of course, correct; but it is easy to fall into the same trap in which these leaders found themselves. Their downfall was relying on their own strength and experiences instead of seeking God for direction.

There are four observations in this passage that drive home the need not to get caught up in what I think are the right experiences or qualifications. God has impressed upon me this strong message for my own life, that when I try to lead in my own strength or experience, this will be the result of my leadership.

1. THE LEADERS AND/OR PROPHETS WERE SAYING, "This is what the Lord says." God emphatically stated to them that He "did not say any such thing!" The leaders were giving instructions out of their own imaginations or thoughts. How many times have we as leaders said just exactly that, when God really didn't affirm anything of the sort to us? But because we have a position of influence and authority, people will take us at our word. We have to be *extremely* careful as leaders using this phraseology. It would be better to say something like this, "I have this impression about your situation, and you can pray about it and see if it would be true in your own spirit, but I just wanted to give you something to think about."

2. FOLLOWING THEIR OWN SPIRITS. The passage goes on to say that the leaders were like jackals wandering around in groups in the desert. Do you know what a jackal does for a living? A jackal moves around in packs and feeds on dead flesh. What a powerful visual for us as leaders. Are we moving around feeding on dead things? Idols, past experiences, our knowledge, wisdom of the world, and then calling ourselves

leaders? Are we "saying this is of the Lord" and imparting lifeless words to our followers? I shudder to think of the consequences of myself giving away something that is dead rather than something that is life giving.

3. FAILING TO REPAIR THE CRACKS IN THE WALL. This can mean a couple of things for us as leaders. It can refer to our own emotional, physical, and spiritual health. We just keep covering up, pouring on the whitewash, because we are so busy for God that we don't stop and repair the cracks. Are we just putting a temporary fix over the cracks in our walls?

In my own life some of the cracks that have surfaced through the years that I had to face were relational issues with my extended family, the breakdown of my health when I kept pushing myself beyond my physical and emotional limitations, problems in my marriage, and struggles with my finances.

Stopping long enough to examine my wall has been a necessary learning curve for me; I have learned that I will be most effective as a leader if I am obedient in examining these cracks in my life as they surface and gain my attention. Whitewashing them will only delay the inevitable, and will certainly hinder the ministry God has entrusted to me.

4. LEADING PEOPLE ASTRAY. When we lead in our own strength, we invite the danger of leading others astray, away from God instead of to God. That's exactly what happened in Ezekiel's time. They made claims about God that God had nothing to

do with. This is a serious problem, especially today. What was once seen as clear and concise truth has been watered down to the point of everyone deciding what his or her truth should be. We will be held responsible as leaders for the truth we communicate to others. It keeps me motivated to make sure I am listening to God every step of the way!

Instead of sharing another story of an amazing woman, I want to close this chapter with a simple exercise and time of reflection. Please take an opportunity to stop what you are doing, and if you can, grab your Bible and pen, go to a quiet place, and reflect on these questions.

As honestly as you are able to right now, complete the following:

Which of these four warnings can you identify with?

1. Leading out of your own thoughts

2. Following your own spirits; feeding on dead things

3. Failing to repair the cracks in the wall; nurturing the physical, emotional, and spiritual parts of your being

4. Leading people astray

What step is God asking you to take at this moment? Who can you share this with confidentially that can commit to pray for you? Write out a prayer to God expressing your thoughts.

Dear God . . .

Chapter 11

Leading from the Home Front

LOIS AND EUNICE

"There is eternal influence and power in motherhood."
—JULIE B. BECK

"I looked on child rearing not only as a work of love and duty
but as a profession that was fully as interesting and challenging
as any honorable profession in the world and one that demanded
the best that I could bring to it."
—ROSE KENNEDY

The music was playing "Pomp and Circumstance" as my fellow graduates and I streamed through the auditorium. My friends and families witnessed me walking down the aisle with other students draped in academic regalia. It was the end of a journey. After three years, I finally reached the finish line and was being awarded my master's in leadership degree. As I sat there with my friends, I was overwhelmed with emotion. And wouldn't you know it, I was unprepared for the tears. To tell you the truth, it actually caught me off guard. It was the culmination of my academic pilgrimage, a long, arduous one full of classes, stacks of books to read, tea lattes, chocolate, and bleary-eyed nights writing papers. I could only sit there misty-eyed hoping my nose wouldn't start running because there wasn't a tissue in sight! With immense gratitude I thanked God for all He had allowed me to accomplish. I sensed His delight and His quiet whisper in my soul, "I am so proud of you!"

Going back to school after several decades was at times close to torture, yet at other times it was life-giving. It felt as though I was giving birth again as my mind seemed to develop stretch marks and my heart was deeply challenged in my own practice of leadership and ministry. Returning to university has been a lifelong dream for me. I love to learn. I have an insatiable appetite to read and discover new information and apply it to life. My latent school adventure was no exception. I came to the conclusion that even though I was older than my classmates (not all of them, whew!), my view of learning through the lens of life experience afforded me a fresh perspective on what I was absorbing.

When I started this book, I shared with you my own insecurities of being a leader and feeling inadequate. Many times I have had to fight off the lie of our last myth, I DON'T HAVE ENOUGH EXPERIENCE, as I have wrestled through a myriad of leadership roles. For years I actually believed that academic education would be the answer to those insecurities. I didn't have the opportunity to acquire the education that I so desperately wanted until recently.

I believe God held off on my dream for a few decades because He wanted to teach me in other ways. Do you know what I learned? I learned that academia alone isn't the answer to stepping up to lead. I learned the opposite. I learned that knowledge, practically applied with life experience (both our failure and success), is what renews the heart and becomes the crowning piece of transformational servant leadership. I think I knew that deep down, but it hadn't made the 12-inch journey from my head to my heart. My professors and classmates helped me to examine that space between my head and my heart that I hadn't explored. I found myself reinventing my theology of leadership, shedding the lies I had believed about myself and God as I dug deep reading and writing about what I believed. But one of the greatest lessons I learned from gaining my degree was in facing my own fears and insecurities and realizing that it is actually a good place to be for me to grow up into an effective servant leader. I discovered that it has little to do with feeling whether I have enough experience to do what God has called me to do.

Graduating Milestones

Those tears during the graduation ceremony that caught me off guard reminded me of other moments in life of "graduation-like" events I've encountered when I have felt the myth of I DON'T HAVE ENOUGH EXPERIENCE. This one was academic; others have been less academic and less formal. I like to call them milestone graduations or defining moments when something shifts and takes root in my heart as a marker that commemorates something of value on my life journey. Most of the time it seems they have to do with life learning in the context of relationship choices. that have the possibility of altering the circumstances of relationships. One of the monumental milestones has been in making the choice to be a mom; not only in the sense of birthing and raising our three sons but also in making a conscious choice to be not just their mom and caregiver, but loving them with intentional purpose with the prayer that they would grow up to be remarkable human beings who could be in love with Jesus and be world changers.

Never has the myth of I Don't Have Enough Experience plagued me more than being a mom—even more than being a leader! God had plans in developing my leadership character and it was in the season of raising our three boys. At first, being a mother was a task. I hate to admit this, but I approached motherhood as a to-do list with an end goal in sight. Although I love my three boys dearly, in many ways for the first several years, I saw them as a project to finish so I could move on and do the next important task that God might ask me to do. I was so driven to make a difference, I wanted my life to count and I just didn't see it all through the eyes of motherhood. There was just one problem—Jeremy, Jordan, and Jason weren't projects, they were little people, little souls that had been entrusted to me to nurture, love, and influence as the primary caregiver.

Not at any time did this become clearer to me than when I was asked to be the worship leader at our church. Our boys at the time were nine, three, and two. Our church was growing and

I jumped in with both feet developing our worship program. I taught workshops, trained vocalists, created worship band teams, and led weekly myself. I might mention to you that I also was leading another ministry. It was a seasonal ministry so it didn't overlap until later in the year. About nine months into my new role, I started fraying at the edges.

My husband was the associate pastor in our church. Sunday mornings we went our separate ways, as he had to be at church earlier. I was like a single mom getting the kids ready, dragging them to church in time so I could be there to practice with the band and then lead worship for the two services. Our oldest son, Jeremy, had the chore of watching his toddler brothers until Sunday School started. Even though he was willing, I could sense that it was challenging for him as a nine-year-old to have that responsibility. He has teased me from time to time that he helped to raise his brothers. I am sure he got that impression solely from the times I subjected him to carrying more than he should have as a nine-year-old. It was too much; he needed just to be a child and not help to facilitate my pursuits.

By the time we got home from two services, we had all been at church for more than six hours. Sunday afternoons were a disaster. I was crabby, the kids were crabby. Monday was like the day after a nuclear explosion. During the rest of the week I was tired all the time, staying up way too late. Saturday night was spent preparing for the next Sunday. I finally found that I was losing my grip, but I didn't want to admit it.

I was juggling so much that there was no margin left over in my life and it was showing, first at home and eventually in my leadership at church. Taxed beyond my limits, I had a growing sense of failure as a mom and a leader. Although it appeared from the outside that I had it all together, inside I knew I was crumbling if something didn't change.

One weekend, Kevin suggested we evaluate how things were going. He took me away for the day so we could talk; we spent time hiking at one of our favorite spots. He was a wise husband. I think by that point he knew it wouldn't take much to set off a bomb. He gently suggested as we hiked the trail that maybe it wasn't the right season for me to be so involved since we all seemed to be paying dearly. Even though he was very supportive and loved what I was doing, it was obvious it wasn't working.

Now I need to tell you that my husband is no wimp. He is a strong leader with strong opinions, but he exercised the wisdom of Solomon in this case. He observed how much I loved what I was doing. I was flourishing even though things were starting to crack on the home front. He foresaw the danger if I kept going; it would be like an avalanche that if left unchecked could eventually bury our family. So he did something audacious. He asked me to pray. He didn't tell me I had to quit, but simply asked me to pray and ask God whether this was the right role at the right time. He said it was my decision and he would support me whatever I decided.

Don't you hate that? I secretly wished he would just tell me I had to quit, but he knew that if he did, I might be resentful; so he trusted God to speak to me and He did loud and clear. I quit the worship position after praying about it for a few weeks. The minute I did, a rush of relief washed over me. It was at that point that God impressed on me about what I was doing, and it had everything to do with timing. God tenderly reminded me of those three small faces I looked into every single day, that they were my ministry in that season. All the passion I had poured into the worship God asked me instead to pour into leading and loving my boys. It was like a boulder of realization fell into my heart. Time seemed to stand still for a few moments as the reality sank in—these little boys were my legacy. These boys will remember all I do to make them the top priority and ministry in my life. Everyone else at the time would forget the workshops I led, the songs I sang, the vocalists I trained, but my boys would remember whether I poured my passion into being their mother.

Now please hear me. I am not saying that being a mom means you can't do anything else; in fact, I really believe that a mom should be pursuing her dreams and nurturing her gifts while she has children, but skillfully and with wisdom. I think it is vitally important and I believe the best way to show our children how to serve is to lead by example and involve them when we can. Jordan, our middle son, reminded me of this in a conversation I had with him recently. He told me that one of his fondest memories was when we involved him and his brothers in serving together at church during our Christmas Dessert Theatre productions. He remembered hanging out with the other families painting sets, running errands, eating pizza, and staying late nights at church preparing for the event. In his words, he said, "Church was fun as a kid." We worked together and that was the point he was helping me to see.

Our children are a part of a very momentous season and

they are our legacy. We can't have a do-over if we change our minds. We can still lead from the home front, but it just has to look different, and it is unique to every woman and every family. Anne-Marie Slaughter in her article "Why Women Still Can't Have It All" shares the perspective of how women are caught in the notion that we can do it all. Slaughter had her dream job at the US State Department in Washington, DC; and though she was climbing the ladder of success, she felt she was missing something, her family. Her husband backed her up, but she found herself simply wanting to be home to make pancakes for her family and attend her son's games without the pressure of her career. She lived at home only on the weekends and worked away from home during the week. She was torn in her desire to pursue her passion and yet be available for her kids. Whether it is making a decision about how much to work or how much to be involved in the community or at church, evaluating your individual situation is paramount to learning to lead effectively from the home front.

I want to be sensitive to the moms who don't have a choice but to work outside the home and are taxed beyond their limits due to economic stress or find themselves left alone as single parents. If you are one of these women, you are among my heroes. You have a tough job and I know there is little margin to negotiate. I believe that God can help you make a way to sort it out so that you, too, can lead effectively from the home front. My encouragement would be to tap into the resources your church might have to offer.

PLEASE PERMIT: This is an aside and we won't derail our focus, however, need to do a better job in our churches of supporting our single parents. One of the churches in our region does an incredible job of taking care of their single parents; they are a blessing to our city. Wouldn't it be great if we could follow their example and give these weary parents the break they deserve so they too could find the time to explore their own passions and dreams?

BACK TO THE MAIN POINT: What might be your boulder of realization that God drops into your heart?

Godly Influence

Timothy might be the greatest biblical example of a man who was raised by a godly mother-daughter duo: Lois, his grand-mother, and Eunice, his mother. The Bible says of this dynamic team and their influence over Timothy: "I am reminded of your sincere faith, which first lived in your grandmother Lois and in your mother Eunice and, I am persuaded, now lives in you also" (2 Timothy 1:5). In another reference, Paul charged Timothy and reminded him of his spiritual heritage from these two women when he said, "And how from infancy you have known the holy scriptures which are able to make you wise for salvation through faith in Christ Jesus" (2 Timothy 3:15). Their influence was sym-bolic as they raised Timothy from a baby to love and fear the

Lord and His Word. Our influence is powerful over our children. It doesn't go unnoticed; rather it is where we exercise some of our most inspiring leadership.

Another example that points to the power of parental influence is the story of King Hezekiah. Although his father Ahaz was an evil king who proliferated idol worship in the nation, his mother quite possibly was the godly influence over his life. Abijah, Hezekiah's mother, was the daughter of Zechariah, who was one of the high priests in Jerusalem at the Temple. Quite contrary to his father, the Bible says that King Hezekiah "did what was right in the eyes of the Lord" (2 Chronicles 29:2). Hezekiah sought to purify the land from his father's idol worship and he restored the Temple. Within the first month of his reign he set out to consecrate what had been desecrated. His heart was set on pleasing the Lord throughout his lifetime. It wouldn't be hard to debate that his primary influence probably came from his mother. Abijah led from the home front and a whole nation was blessed.

Never-Ending

I have found that influencing family doesn't end with being a mom. The cycle continues as a grandmother. I have yet another part of my legacy to fulfill. I can be like Lois and influence my grandchildren in a way that far outlasts my own earthly life. The role of grandmother, too, has become a priority and a value that I choose to work into my schedule. It is about making a commitment to my grandchildren.

At this season one of the most incredible joys I have is to watch Jeremy's wife, Emily, embrace motherhood. I can remember when we first talked about her future to pursue a career before she married Jeremy. When they had their kids, they made a very difficult decision to try and live on one income so Emily could stay home with the children. In order to make it work, they both had to give up some desires. She had been a very successful teacher, teaching Spanish in a private school. Some would see giving up her career to stay home with her kids as a negative. But at a closer look, she didn't really give it up because she demonstrates the same, if not greater, passion in nurturing and loving her boys. It shows and she is content. I rarely if ever hear her complain about being a mom. She soaks it all up and captures the moments both hilarious and challenging, making memories that are priceless.

There has been no greater reward for me than to learn leadership in the life lab of being a mom to my sons. I didn't see it in the midst of the dirty diapers, long days of laundry, dishes, flu bugs, homework, and endless driving. It came much later. One of the best Mother's Days I ever had came in the form of three separate cards from each of my boys, each of them not knowing what the other had written. To this day I cherish those cards more than any gift they have ever given me. In each card was expressed the same theme in their own way. They shared their gratefulness that I had made them my first priority outside of God and their dad. They thanked me for teaching them to love Jesus and praying for them. They cheered me on with my gifts now that they each had left home. They encouraged me to pursue my dreams and told me how proud they were of me. I cried that day and have saved those cards as a reminder that my decision those years ago to lead from the home front was one of the most important decisions I have ever made.

I can't tell you how many graduations, weddings, sports games, and ministry events that I as a mother have been privileged to share in through the years. One of the greatest honors for me was to have my adult sons and their wives cheer me on as I crossed the platform to receive my degree, fulfilling a lifetime dream. The role reversal seemed odd and felt funny. But today they are celebrating their mom in her pursuits. They are rallying as I write this book and have thoughtfully listened as I have bounced ideas off them and subjected them to reading chapters and giving feedback.

It took a long time, but I finally got it. And I know now that the best learning climate I could ever be in happened right in the four walls of our home, living it out with my husband, being a mom to our three boys, loving them through Jesus. I didn't do it perfectly; in fact, I made enormous mistakes; but by God's outrageous grace and prayer they somehow found their own spiritual footing. I am blessed as I watch them today be the remarkable world changers I prayed they would be as they live out their own faith. It has been so worth it!

God, thank You for allowing me to learn what true influence is right from my own home. Give me grace to accept and embrace each season You've given me. Help me to celebrate

the moments, to not rush ahead of Your plans, and to engage in each experience. Help me to open up my heart and align my thinking with the truth of Your Word when it comes to loving my family. Give me wisdom, Lord, to balance my home in pursuing my gifts and talents. Help me to know how much margin I need and what my limits are. Lead me, Jesus, to be led from the home front for Your glory and honor!

Chapter 12

Leading in the Twilight Years

ANNA

"That man never grows old who keeps a child in his heart."
—RICHARD STEELE

*"The minute a man ceases to grow, no matter what his
years, that minute he begins to be old."*
—WILLIAM JAMES

Driving out of the filthy, polluted streets of Phnom Penh
and into the countryside was a relief. For several days we
had been ministering in and out of the capital city of Cambodia
and the stress of noise and pollution was wearing on our team.
Today was a significant day. We were going to have the privilege
of meeting Marie Ens at her Place of Rescue compound. As soon
as we drove up, our surroundings spoke of beauty, peace, and
love. The Place of Rescue is a community of hope that cares for
more than 250 children in the orphanage and AIDS center; it has
homes for abandoned pregnant girls and abandoned grannies.
Part of the AIDS center houses the parents, mostly women, who

have contracted AIDS. They live in small, clean thatched huts in which adults young and old ravaged by the disease of AIDS can die with dignity. Some have contracted the disease from their husbands who have slept with prostitutes and have long since left them. Marie told us that most if not all Cambodian men sleep with prostitutes and they can acquire sex as easily as buying a drink and for as little as two dollars.

Many come to the Place of Rescue after being left to die on the streets of the city and surrounding areas. Unable to care for themselves, Marie and her team transport them to the Refuge of Hope to give them medical care, a comfortable bed, clean water, and food. Most of all they extend the love of Jesus to them and preserve their dignity. There is new hope in recent years because of the free antiretroviral drugs that are available which allow them to be able to feel well enough to work in the gardens, sew, clean, and work with the babies. In addition to the Place of Rescue, there is in the city of Phnom Penh a dormitory called the House of New Dreams where the older children have the opportunity to attend university and learn a trade. With this preparation they can launch a successful career, break out of the cycle of poverty, and help others do the same.

Children who lovingly call her *Makyeah*, which means grandma in the Khmer language of Cambodia, surround Marie. She is a woman of average stature; wispy, white hair; a smile; and an embrace that instantly makes you feel at home. The Place of Rescue breathes hope. Miracles happen at Place of Rescue because Marie believes in the healing power of God's love in the midst of a poverty-stricken country. She seeks to bring a bit of heaven to Place of Rescue with acres that burst with vegetable gardens, flowers of all varieties, food, shelter, and education carved out of a destitute society with little or no infrastructure.

Cambodia is seeking to rebuild after a horrific genocide led by the Khmer Rouge in the late 1970s. Before this time, Marie and her husband had come to Cambodia in the early 1960s as missionaries. They were thriving and grew to love the Khmer people. As the country's unrest grew, they left, moved to France, and continued to work with Cambodians that had immigrated to that region. Praying for their beloved country, they continued to be connected to the hearts of the Cambodian people.

In the early 1990s Marie found herself a widow and departed to go back home. She then later returned to Cambodia in 1994 with the Christian and Missionary Alliance (CMA) Mission. She came in contact with her first AIDS patient at a hospital and began to realize the devastation of the crisis and her responsibility to act, but it seemed overwhelming. She worked with the CMA for 6 years until they asked her to retire.

The irony of her story is that Marie wasn't ready to retire. After working in partnership with her husband for nearly 50 years, she wasn't sure what she could offer or how she could serve as a single woman. Her heart, however, was drawn back over and over again to Cambodia and specifically the AIDS crisis. Officially being labeled a retired missionary didn't block her determination.

As she sought the Lord she came upon the story of Abraham and heard the Lord say to her heart, "Grow old along with me, the best is yet to be." This spry, white-haired woman believed the

Lord still had something for her to do in Cambodia despite the request for her to retire from the mission. She returned on her own in 2001 and embraced a new beginning of God blessing her with spiritual motherhood in the form of ministering to widows and orphans ravaged by the cruel disease of AIDS in her beloved country. Marie didn't allow age to stand in her way. She decided she would go anyway, depending on her retirement savings and trusting God for support to step out and realize the dream that she sensed was clearly from God. The AIDS center opened in 2002, and the first children came to live in the orphanage in 2004.

Marie could have easily slipped into the comfortable retirement years in her prairie town of Regina, Saskatchewan. But she couldn't ignore the ache in her soul to respond to God's call. God has given her strength in these twilight years and she still is dreaming big dreams for God at nearly 80 years old! Marie's determination is both inspiring and contagious. Neither age nor thoughts of "I DON'T HAVE ENOUGH EXPERIENCE" are barriers to God's call to rise up and lead. Even if we haven't led anything on our own, if God plants a dream in our heart, He will fulfill it no matter what our age, status, or resources. Did I neglect to mention that Marie gets phenomenal support all around the world? She prays the vision and God has provided in incredible ways for the Place of Rescue.

Marie has used what I like to call her "life equity." All her seasoned years of nurturing children; teaching; partnering with her husband; being a faithful wife, mother, and friend prepared her to love the Cambodian people in the Place of Rescue. She was experienced in love and relationships and, therefore, could extend the grace and love of Jesus. She didn't necessarily have all the experience in developing the ministry of Place of Rescue and all the red tape involved—acquiring land legally, running a nonprofit, and successfully caring for the medical needs of the children and parents—but she had faith that God would bring others to help facilitate what God has asked her to do. And He has done exactly that! I marvel at Marie's vision. Since my visit in 2007, she has built the House of New Dreams in the city and acquired more property and buildings to care for more orphans. I remember sitting at her lunch table and her sharing the next part of the dream. I believe God has honored her faith and accelerated the process of acquiring land, buildings, and staff by granting her favor.

By now you may be thinking, *I am beginning the last years of my life. God can't possibly have anything for me. Let the younger ones take up the banner of leadership.* To that I would say a hearty *no!* Age is relative in God's sight. He takes our life equity and builds on it to accomplish His purposes in our lives, regardless of what we think our experience can do. Our responsibility is to listen as Marie did and not settle for the comfortable.

A Life of Worship

Anna, in the Book of Luke, was also in her twilight years. Her story takes place in Luke 2. She served at the Temple and had been married only seven years before she became a widow. She dedicated her life to worshipping and serving in the Temple in Jerusalem. She was known as a prophetess in her advanced years. She was committed to fasting and praying. Age was no barrier to Anna. God has a way of making His purposes clear at any age if we live a life of worship and surrender to Him with Anna as our example. Her life was full because she was full of love for Jehovah. This is her story.

> *Anna, a prophet, was also there in the Temple. She was the daughter of Phanuel from the tribe of Asher, and she was very old. Her husband died when they had been married only seven years. Then she lived as a widow to the age of eighty-four. She never left the Temple but stayed there day and night, worshiping God with fasting and prayer. She came along just as Simeon was talking with Mary and Joseph, and she began praising God. She talked about the child to everyone who had been waiting expectantly for God to rescue Jerusalem* (Luke 2:36–38 NLT).

Anna probably never dreamed that her reward would be that she would actually get to see the promised Messiah, Jesus Christ. Her life embodied worship even unto the end of her life. Anna didn't allow the pain and suffering of being a widow to rob her of her joy for God. Her joy was met in fulfilling God's call in the Temple and it was worthy enough to be noted in the Book of Luke. How many older joyful people do you know? It is quite rare at times to find truly joyful older people. Many are marred with complaining, whining, and sadness. Anna's example speaks to me profoundly in that I want my life to be marked by praise and worship in my twilight years, no matter what I have faced.

So often in our latter years we can be tempted to coast through until the end. Just as Marie and Anna, the key to leading fulfilling twilight years is to be open as we worship, pray, and fast. Never shut our hearts to the things that are important to God—widows, orphans, feeding the poor, giving voice to those who have no voice. It is never too late to start. Cultivating a joyful heart is built a step at a time by serving others no matter what our age. We can all do something even if we have limitations socially, physically, or financially. God can make a way just as He made a way for Marie and her dream of rescuing people who suffer from AIDS. Did she have a big plan or strategy? I doubt it. Her greatest asset in her older years was her faith. She believed God could still do miracles when she began her new ministry even at 60-plus years old! As I write, Marie will be 79 in a few months and she hopes to continue until she is 80. I bet God has another journey for her as she joyfully embraces each step.

God help me intentionally cultivate a joyful heart in all circumstances. I don't want to grow old and be a bitter, resentful, and crabby woman. Help me to trust Your strength instead of my own experiences. Lord, increase my faith as I get older and help me to turn my experiences into expressions of praise.

Chapter 13

Leading Intentionally and Leaving a Godly Legacy

DEBORAH

The Call to Make a Difference

"Some of us have great runways already built for us. If you have one, take off! But if you don't have one, realize it is your responsibility to grab a shovel and build one for yourself and for those who will follow after you."
—Amelia Earhart

"The greatest use of life is to spend it for something that will outlast it."
—William James

Sitting on top of a small bookcase in our guest room is a stand with a very crude plaster plate. The plate has a hand imprint and next to the imprint is etched the name of our son Jordan, scribbled in his fourth-grade handwriting. I decided one day to take it out of the box I have saved for him to display it proudly, partly because recently I find myself in the new season of having adult children and I miss my kids on some days. They are gone, married, and grown up with lives of their own.

The other reason is to remind myself that my life will leave an imprint long after I am gone. I make choices every single day that will determine just what kind of legacy will be left. I have a choice of what kind of legacy I will offer my children, grandchildren, friends, and community. Will I make choices that will outlast my own life? Being a new grandparent has brought this truth home to me. The reality is, if I live a good, long life, I will be fortunate to possibly attend their college graduations and their weddings. If I am really fortunate, I may even get to hold a great-grandbaby. I won't be around forever, but what I do today will impact the memories my grandchildren will hold in their hearts.

Remember our talk about fairy tales at the beginning of our journey through this book? They all end with living happily ever after. In reality we don't always live happily ever after, even if we make the right choices. The real test in finishing this life and leaving a godly legacy is our choices in the midst of the not-so-happily-ever-after seasons.

These are difficult days. Even tonight as I am writing these words, the East Coast of the United States is being pounded by a storm unprecedented in history, causing widespread destruction. Not far back in our memories linger the devastation of Japan, Indonesia, and Hurricane Katrina. On the home front, people are continuing to lose jobs, homes, and their sense of hope. We are experiencing a shakedown of what is most important in life and it is sobering. I know it has me more eternity-minded and paying more attention to my choices. This has an impact on how I view my legacy.

What kind of world will we leave for future generations? What really is the foundation of our society as we witness the familiar moorings being torn away? What is the core value that our communities rest on? At one time, the center of a community was the church. We visited Charleston, South Carolina, on an anniversary trip. On a city tour we were told that no building was allowed to be built higher than the tallest church steeple. It was a designated symbol that marked the core of life at that time in the mid-nineteenth century. The tour guide mentioned that the ships would navigate their way into the city harbor by the church steeple. Now the tallest buildings that reign over our cities are financial centers. Our tour guide said that one could tell the infrastructure of society by the type of buildings that tower over the landscape. Interesting how we have moved ahead in the name of progress. It motivates me all the more to be faithful in seeking to live out a godly legacy.

A Leader Ahead of Her Time

Several thousand years ago there was a nation similar to ours—a nation in crisis. It was said of this nation, "Men did what was right in their own eyes." Doesn't that describe who we are today? Every person doing what they think is best and right for them?

The nation I am referring to is the nation of Israel during the period of the Judges. Moses and Joshua, who led Israel out of bondage from Egypt, had long since left the scene. The victories and miracles God had done for the children of Israel had faded. They found themselves in crisis and lacking leadership. They had walked away from God, after He had so mercifully delivered them from their enemies and brought peace not only to their lives but their land as well. But because they failed to acknowledge God's goodness, they became subject to the stronger nations and rulers around them. They became oppressed. Then God chose to raise up Deborah to remind them that by following God, they could live in freedom and victory.

We were introduced to Deborah in Chapter 8: Leading Outside the Box. In a time and culture where women weren't very highly regarded, God saw the heart of this brilliant and wise woman to stand in the gap for the nation of Israel. Her story is found in Judges 4. Here is a segment:

> *Deborah, the wife of Lappidoth, was a prophet who was judging Israel at that time. She would sit under the Palm of Deborah, between Ramah and Bethel in the hill country of Ephraim, and the Israelites would go to her for judgment. One day she sent for Barak son of Abinoam, who lived in Kedesh in the land of Naphtali. She said to him, "This is what the Lord, the God of Israel, commands you: Call out 10,000 warriors from the tribes of Naphtali and Zebulun at Mount Tabor. And I will call out Sisera, commander of Jabin's army, along with his chariots and warriors, to the Kishon River. There*

> *I will give you victory over him. "Barak told her,*
> *"I will go, but only if you go with me."*
>
> *"Very well," she replied, "I will go with you. But*
> *you will receive no honor in this venture, for the*
> *Lord's victory over Sisera will be at the hands of a*
> *woman" (Judges 4:4–9 NLT).*

As we learned in chapter 8, she wasn't referring to herself in verse 9, but rather Jael whom God used to accomplish the victory.

Why did God choose Deborah? I believe God chose Deborah because she believed God, and she exercised incredible faith, concluding that God wanted to restore Israel and to restore faith in the living God they had walked away from. God saw a woman who looked beyond the crisis and tumultuous times of her country and said, "I have the living God on my side and with Him everything is possible!" Her response to Barak proved her faith. God is pleased when we believe and trust Him. I think that God saw that Deborah not only believed, had faith, but that she placed her inexplicable trust in the living God.

HOPE AND YOUR IMPRINT

What happens when we hear all the bad news about our city, our country, our nation, and our world? If you are like me, you tend to lose hope! You might be thinking this is a depressing way to finish this book. It may be, but my prayer is that after reading the stories of ordinary women in these pages and dispelling the myths, that you and I would respond with greater intention and purpose. We give up so easily today because our culture makes things so easy for us. Our spiritual muscles are like gelatin. They have been conditioned, and when we can't figure it out, or life smacks us sideways, we give up hope. Hopelessness breeds discouragement, despair, and depression. And then we no longer have the drive or motivation to think that we can make a difference because the needs are so great.

I look to Deborah when my feelings are out of control. *She is my heroine.* Against overwhelming odds, Deborah was a woman whom God used to turn things around. And I believe that God wants to do the same through you and me today. We need to believe God more than we can humanly express. We need to trust that He desires to use each one of us to leave an imprint, a godly imprint that will last long after we are gone.

The handprint I have in my guest room isn't just a remembrance of a child's hand in some plaster. It is to me an imprint in my heart, an imprint of my hopes and dreams to make a difference. It is an imprint to leave a godly legacy. Jordan's imprint reflects my longing to make a lasting mold of hope as dark as today seems. *There is hope*, and I believe God is raising up a mighty army of women, princess warriors to make a difference in a dark and dying world.

As we wrap up our journey in these pages, I would like to give you a few thoughts to encourage you to stand in the gap and know for certain that you can make a lasting imprint for the kingdom of God.

The first is the reminder we talked about earlier. Learn to be little. Learn to be small so God can be big in your life, as

Jill Briscoe reminded us. Learn to step down, instead of wanting to step up. As a leader it is tempting to want to step up, be recognized, design great programs, and accumulate accolades. As I have already alluded to, I have just come through a dark season of wilderness in which God gave me the opportunity to step away to chisel at my character and prepare me for the next adventure. It was a time chosen by God because I have come to understand the depths of His love and grace. I have reexamined and turned inside out most everything I have believed in since I was a child. The crisis dictated it, and though it has been an arduous journey, it has been necessary. God prunes those He loves. In the midst, God has whispered to me, "Learn to be little, learn to be more humble, more content, more satisfied only in Me."

The second is to *push through the obstacles*. In other words, don't make the obstacles your focus. God is still looking for ordinary men and women to stand in the gap for their families, churches, communities, cities, and nations. He isn't looking for superqualified, highly educated, or even highly experienced servants of God. He is looking for women who will believe that He can use our simple, ordinary lives to make a difference where we live.

I am sure that when Deborah was a little girl she wasn't thinking, *Oh, someday, I am going to lead an army into victory for God*. Or even, *I am going to be a judge and ruler over the nation of Israel*. I believe she possibly grew up dreaming ordinary dreams that any little girl would dream. And somehow, as she continued to commit her way and will to the Lord, He led her on a journey to make her imprint, her lasting legacy, for such a time as this because of her faithfulness. She ended up changing the course of history.

I believe God wants to do that for each one of us, not just for Deborah or Mother Teresa, Beth Moore, Priscilla Shirer, or any of our heroes. He is leading each one of us on a similar journey, a journey that will encompass our dreams and hopes for the future, a journey that would come together with who God designed us to be and converge with His purposes to make a difference right where He has assigned us in our sphere of influence.

Ephesians 3:14–21 is my mantra for hope that God has destined me to make a difference. I just need to hang on and claim these promises, and I extend to you an invitation to do the same.

For this reason I kneel before the Father, from whom every family in heaven and on earth derives its name. I pray that out of his glorious riches he may strengthen you with power through his Spirit in your inner being, so that Christ may dwell in your hearts through faith. And I pray that you, being rooted and established in love, may have power, together with all the Lord's holy people, to grasp how wide and long and high and deep is the love of Christ, and to know this love that surpasses knowledge—that you may be filled to the measure of all the fullness of God. Now to him who is able to do immeasurably more than all we ask or imagine, according to his power that is at work within us, to him be glory in the church and in Christ

Jesus throughout all generations, for ever and ever!
Amen (Ephesians 3:14–21).

If these words don't give you and me the confidence we need, then I don't know what will. Think on this with me for a moment. I have a better idea, let's speak it out together these powerful truths. He is able to accomplish more than we could even dare to ask or hope. He is able to do in your life and in mine what we secretly have hidden in our hearts that we may be even afraid to whisper to God or ourselves about. He is able to because of how wide, how deep, how marvelous His love truly is. Our God is able! We need to say "Amen" to these things with a loud voice!

What keeps you and me from believing these truths, making us fall into our own little heap of self and saying, "I am nothing special, I am just ordinary," believing the myths? I am talking about doing extraordinary things for God in your sphere of influence—with your children, your co-workers, your community, wherever God has placed you, whatever He has placed you in. You see, God has some wet plaster for you in your home with your kids, your workplace, your church, your community to make a lasting godly imprint for Him. Yes, it may be ordinary, but God goes wild in His extravagant ways to empower us when we are willing with abandoned faith to believe Him, to take risks, and live the adventure He calls to us to live. It is then that we can truly leave our imprint on the generations. Will you believe Him and shatter the myths that keep you from moving forward?

The thing that keeps us from believing we actually can leave an imprint and having faith is allowing the little lies that Satan has begun from the beginning of time to deceive us in believing other than the truth—that God loves us and has our best interests in mind. Satan's strategy hasn't changed since he tempted Adam and Eve in the Garden of Eden. He wants to keep us from dreaming dreams and acting on those dreams for God. The devil wants to keep us insecure, inadequate, and wrapped up in guilt, shame, depression, anger, bitterness, and bondage! Simply put, he is out to alienate and isolate us from God. And we are still falling for it—when we keep believing the myths.

What if Deborah had responded to God in that way? "Oh God, I am just a mother and a wife here in Israel. No woman has ever been in this place. Who me, lead the Israelites? They won't listen to me, why would they listen to me?"

She had a supernatural assignment, a God-given destiny, and a holy presence about her. That is why she was most likely able to break the cultural barrier between men and women in those days. Deborah had plenty of obstacles to overcome. She had a nation that had walked away from God. She had a commander in chief of the army that had little faith in what God had called him to do. It seemed impossible, but God was her strength and she acted on what she thought and believed.

Erwin McManus in his book *The Barbarian Way* gives the premise that we here in North America have made Christianity too comfortable; we are too soft and have domesticated what it means to be a follower of Christ. We don't take risks; we are too self-sufficient. The time has come for radical Christianity and who like Deborah will believe that God wants to penetrate the hearts of our communities and our cities and world.

I am calling you and me to believe something different at this moment, to step over the obstacles in our lives in Jesus' name. We have a job to do, and God is looking for women who will rise up and take the challenge. Women who will shatter the myths that keep us from leaving our imprint, once and for all!

This is my dream for the women I love and meet. I have a dream for my city, my country, and the nations. God is calling us to stand together as women with the courage to lead. Will you join me?

Nonprofit Ministries

AIDS and Orphans in Cambodia—Place of Rescue, Marie Ens, placeofrescue.org

Sex Slavery—Frontline for Justice, frontlineforjustice.org

Homelessness and Poverty—NightShift Street Ministries, MaryAnne Connor, nightshiftministries.org

Christ-Centered 12-Step Program—Freedom Session International, freedomsession.com, Ken and Bonnie Dyck

Faith-Based Residential Program Serving Young Women Caught in Life-Controlling Issues—Mercy Ministries, Nancy Alcorn, mercyministries.com

Bibliography

Andrews, Andy. *Traveler's Gift: Seven Decisions That Determine Success*. Nashville: Thomas Nelson, 2005.

Manning, Brennan. *Ruthless Trust: The Ragamuffin's Path to God*. New York: Harper Collins, 2002.

Scazzero, Peter. *Emotionally Healthy Spirituality: Unleash a Revolution of Your Life in Christ*. Nashville: Thomas Nelson, 2011.

Kent, Carol. *A New Kind of Normal: Hope Filled Choices When Life Turns Upside Down*. Nashville: Thomas Nelson, 2007.

McManus, Erwin. *The Barbarian Way: Unleash the Untamed Faith Within*. Nashville: Thomas Nelson, 2005.

Briscoe, Jill. *The Deep Place Where Nobody Goes: Conversations with God on the Steps of My Soul*. Oxford, UK: Monarch Books, 2005.

Slaughter, A. M. "Why Women Still Can't Have It All." *The Atlantic Magazine,* July/August 2012. http://www.theatlantic.com /magazine/archive/2012/07/why-women-still-cant-have-it -all/309020/2 (accessed July 7, 2012).

Quotes from goodreads.com/quotes

New Hope® Publishers is a division of WMU®, an international organization that challenges Christian believers to understand and be radically involved in God's mission. For more information about WMU, go to wmu.com. More information about New Hope books may be found at NewHopeDigital.com. New Hope books may be purchased at your local bookstore.

Use the QR reader on your
smartphone to visit us online at
NewHopeDigital.com

If you've been blessed by this book, we would like to hear your story. The publisher and author welcome your comments and suggestions at: newhopereader@wmu.org.

Resources to *Encourage* and *Empower* Your Walk with Christ!

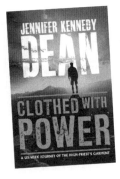

Clothed with Power
A Six-Week Journey to Freedom, Power, and Peace
JENNIFER KENNEDY DEAN
ISBN-10: 1-59669-373-8 • ISBN-13: 978-1-59669-373-9 • N134114 $14.99
*DVD study also available

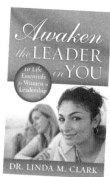

Awaken the Leader in You
10 Essentials for Women in Leadership
DR. LINDA M. CLARK
ISBN-10: 1-59669-221-9 • ISBN-13: 978-1-59669-221-3 • N084144 $12.99

Set Apart
A Six-Week Study of the Beatitudes
JENNIFER KENNEDY DEAN
ISBN-10: 1-59669-263-4 • ISBN-13: 978-1-59669-263-3 • N104132 $14.99
*DVD study also available

Lost on a Familiar Road
Allowing God's Love to
Free Your Mind for the Journey
KIMBERLY SOWELL
ISBN-10: 1-59669-360-6 • ISBN-13: 978-1-59669-360-9 • N134103 $14.99
eDevotional also available!

Available in bookstores everywhere. For information about these books or our authors visit NewHopeDigital.com. Experience sample chapters, podcasts, author interviews and more! Download the New Hope app for your iPad, iPhone, or Android!